Cyber 24/7:
Risks, Leadership
and Sharing

Sound advice for the Board, C-Suite, and non-technical executives

---

Peter L. ODell

Cyber 24/7:
Risks, Leadership, and Sharing

ISBN: **978-1495206276**

Printed in USA by Amazon CreateSpace

Introduction

Cyber security is on everyone's mind; the headlines have been screaming the news about Target and other retail breaches in the last few weeks of 2013. Organizations of all sizes are feeling the pressure to do more, but what to do?

This book examines the risks in the current and future realm of cyber-attacks, the leadership elements necessary to mobilize the entire organization and high payoff activities like information sharing that can help you be more prepared and proactive.

The content is aimed specifically at board of directors, C-Suite executives, and non-technical managers. Chief Information Officers and Chief Information Security Officers will benefit from increased awareness of the organization, and IT staffers will understand a wider scope of the issues around preparing and defending an organization's prized information. Explanations should be understandable without a deep technical background.

We will examine the "people" issues of a strong cyber defense; assembling the right talent pool, and organizing them to be more effective in activities that will protect the organization from a wide range of potential harm inflictors – nation states, cyber criminals, and teenagers with talent and time on their hands.

I will answer some pressing questions that have come up at a number of presentations with senior leadership from many different organizations:

- How big is this risk? Can I handle it with my other organizational liabilities?
- How did we get into this situation?
- What can the board do to oversee our cyber efforts?
- What should senior management do on a daily basis to help prevent attacks/breaches?
- How should my internal team be configured and allocated?
- Who should I turn to for outside help?
- What can I do proactively to prevent attacks and respond better when an attack occurs?
- Why and how do I share information with trusted partners and the government?
- What is the government doing to help organizations be more secure?
- Are there accepted best practices that I should be following?
- How do I stay up to date in relation to the flood of information about cyber security?
- When are things going to get better?
- What are the future trends I need to worry about?

A unified approach will be a central theme; cyber defense is not an isolated Information Technology problem to be delegated down to the server room or to the network geeks; leadership has to set a "tone at the top" that makes everyone aware and cooperative toward a common sense and evolving set of cyber hygiene items – those things you have to do every day to insure a simple mistake or lack of maintenance doesn't cause a big problem.

The world has reaped the benefits of automated computing on a large scale for only 50-odd years, shorter than many of our lifetimes. During this fantastic period in man's history, computing's capabilities and impacts have been continually accelerating and new information technology methods have evolved almost daily. The early days of timesharing on costly mainframes were augmented by less expensive minicomputers in the 70's. The introduction of the personal computer in the early 80's spawned an entirely new generation of applications and capabilities. Today's mobile and tablet based computing is amazing, yet still primitive. Think about what the state of the art was when you were a child – my situation was a party phone line and manual addition/subtraction. We are truly in the middle of a burgeoning information age.

In the background during the 80's, the Internet was moving from a government and university science project to a worldwide capability, gaining exponential growth with the creation of the World Wide Web and browser technology first commercialized by NetScape. Today, cloud computing has moved into the mainstream, and we are seeing an emerging Internet of Things (IOT) where billions of sensors will create even bigger data streams for analysis and real time situational awareness. On the innovation and productivity fronts, the past has been stunning and the future looks equally bright.

Regrettably, this rapid, global expansion has created vulnerabilities for a wide variety of intruders who want to steal your organization's information, harm your reputation and brands, disrupt your communications, compromise your customers and a host of other intrusive and illegal activities. This cyber threat has become the top risk that many organizations face – governments, corporations, nonprofits, small business and individuals alike. Vendors are scrambling to upgrade their software's security capabilities. An entire new industry is rising out of the cyber security problem, selling hardware, software, advice, remediation services and a continuing stream of new cyber defenses. It's imperative that your organization take this threat seriously and respond in real time, with leadership coming from the highest levels of the organization.

You have the responsibility to help your organization overcome these challenges. No matter what your specific role, there are important aspects you should understand and act upon. This book will highlight those elements and the best places to find real time information and assistance. We'll look at sharing, an underutilized defense against attackers – hard, but growing in effectiveness. There is an extensive government effort happening globally, and many consortiums and non-profits are working to increase awareness, readiness and response. Finally, I'll point the way to the future which will be here very quickly.

I'm confident the world will mobilize and mitigate this severe problem around cyber security – the severity of the threat leaves us little choice if we're going to survive and thrive as a global economy. Like many other risk elements the world has faced for thousands of years, this threat will never go away completely, but we will learn to largely contain the problem. Continual vigilance and adaptability by industry and government will be important, and a global approach to defense and law enforcement crucial to containing the rapid expansion of cyber-attacks.

The Boy Scout Motto applies to your cyber posture: "Be Prepared". Best wishes for a safer journey.

About the Author

Pete ODell is a business and technology consultant who lives in Alexandria, Virginia. He has been involved with information technology and business for over 25 years, working for large companies like Autodesk, Digital Equipment Corporation, Microsoft, and Micro Warehouse. He has been involved in multiple startup efforts including Swan Island Networks, Upgrade Corporation of America and Online Interactive. He has been president of a high-growth software company, Chief Information Officer of several large and small corporations, and Chief Operating Officer for multiple startups.

At Swan Island Networks, he had extensive interaction with the U.S. Government in the areas of homeland security, information sharing, real time situational awareness and law enforcement. He now consults for a wide range of companies, and is on the global advisory board for BucketDream.com, www.bucketdream.com, an exciting new enterprise launching in 2014. He is also part of NextLevel www.nextlevel.com, a growing Northwest executive and board services firm.

One of Pete's key skills is the communications and interface between technical groups and non-technical executives and board members. He's presented at National Association of Corporate Directors meetings about cyber security. He firmly believes that technologists must make a far better effort to translate the complexity and acronyms of information technology into understandable and actionable strategies that their executive peers and board members can understand and oversee.

Pete is an avid fly fisherman, an occasional marathoner, and a poor golfer. He volunteers with www.fishingcommunity.org to support our Wounded Heroes with fishing events and classes.

Also by the Author:

Silver Bullets: How Interoperable Data will revolutionize Information Sharing and Transparency, Authorhouse, 2010 for print editions, self-published Kindle edition

Essays on Corporate Governance, Andrew Sherman, Guest Essay: Information Systems and the Chief Information Officer (CIO), Advantage, 2012

The Computer Networking Book, Ventana Press, 1989

Table of Contents

Chapter 1: The Cyber Threat – Where Are We Today?

"Information technology and business are becoming inextricably interwoven. I don't think anybody can talk meaningfully about one without the talking about the other." - Bill Gates

Current version note: This book was written in late 2013 with the intention to refresh the Amazon Kindle version every 3-6 months with updated information about the rapidly changing cyber threat and security space. Contact the author if you don't think you have the latest version.

Our world is under attack – seriously and continually. The attacks are not the aliens arriving, nor a global pandemic disease, but many different organizations and people trying to exploit security weaknesses in the computing systems we've come to rely on in almost every facet of our lives. Organizations with global reach and the largest of governments are one set of targets, falling victim to denial of service attacks and major data breaches. Individuals and small business are another set of victims as identify theft has been a growing problem. Everything in between those two groups makes up the rest of the many targets under attack. The perpetrators range from nation states to teenagers and the attacks from harmless defacement of a website to the theft of national security secrets. If you take nothing else away from this book, just understanding and acting upon the seriousness of this threat might save your organization from a major intrusion and expense.

In the beginning: While there will likely be other stories about the very beginning of cyber security issues, I would submit that the first malware involving the Internet came from Robert Morris, a student at Cornell University. The Morris worm was launched in November 1988 in what was thought to be a science project by Morris (the worm did not do anything devastating or destructive) but quickly spiraled out of control due to a design flaw in his self-replicating code. I was the Director of Information Technology at Autodesk in Sausalito, California, and we had a large software development network of Sun Microsystems workstations running UNIX that were impacted – crashing or completely unresponsive. The response was a rapid, collaborative effort by industry and universities to eliminate the worm from the infected systems and prevent its further spread. Robert Morris was the first individual to be convicted under the Computer Fraud and Abuse Act that had been passed in 1986. The threat has gotten much worse from this innocuous beginning.

Cyber-attacks are a serious risk to all types of organizations and have been growing rapidly over the last decade – in breadth, depth, numbers and complexity. I've included some of the latest information on statistics, trends, attacks vectors, and an industry breakdown toward the end of the chapter, but it's pretty easy to see that the cyber landscape is very dangerous and will stay that way for the foreseeable future. Many of the current problems are dangerous and can inflict great harm, but are known and reasonably visible if you are paying very strict attention. One of the greatest threats comes from combined innovation and agility by the perpetrators of these attacks on a global basis – with the prospect of an even deadlier set of attacks emerging as the attackers gain knowledge and expertise. It is important to keep current and understand the emerging threats.

The price of an attack can be huge. This statistic is from the 2012 Cost of Cyber Crime Study: Ponemon Institute:

"Cyber crimes continue to be costly. We found that the average annualized cost of cyber crime for 60 organizations in our study is $11.6 million per year, with a range of $1.3 million to $58 million. In 2012, the average annualized cost was $8.9 million."

The cyber problem has received much attention over the last several years. Globally, governments and large organizations have been scrambling to put the right measures for combatting attacks into place. Boards of directors have started to become sensitized to the issues and the media has brought the details of many major breaches into the public domain, demonstrating that nobody is safe or above the risk of attack. Overall, things are still very disorganized and chaotic, so assurances of competence and invulnerability should be validated and verified. Don't take anything for granted, or you will be almost certainly disappointed.

"Keep Calm and Carry On": In 1939, the British were facing the wrath of the Nazis – there was the threat and capability for the Germans bombing major British cities, especially London. In light of these expected attack and the impact on the spirit and overall well-being of the British people, this national awareness campaign was created, but was never was deployed. You will occasionally still see a shirt or slogan that has been adapted based on the program and the underlying longevity of this message.   Its important to remember that, despite today's cyber vulnerabilities and attacks, life will go on. One of the best courses for everyone is a calm, deliberate, persistant approach to the overall security goals of the organization. Staying operational and functional are the goals, defeating the outside and inside threats a means toward that goal. Blind panic will not help your organization cope.

A turbulent time: Information Technology has moved from the computer room and the geek squad to virtually every aspect of an organization's operations. New capabilities are being deployed continually – sometimes by formal IT efforts, but other times by departmental efforts that involve skipping around the traditional IT cycle and personnel (this is known as rogue IT efforts). An example of a rogue IT project might be the sales department signing up for a cloud based, Software as a Service, Customer Relationship Management solution, and deliberately keeping IT out of the implementation and deployment. With only a browser and internet access needed, many different web based solutions can suddenly be injected into the mix of applications being utilized inside an organization. This rapid proliferation can mean that many more integration points or "seams" can allow opportunities for intruders to compromise one part of the enterprise system and then transverse across to other, more sensitive areas. A strong security strategy will consider all the different initiatives going on across the organization.

Victims of our own success: In the cyber security space, we're vulnerable on many fronts, each with a different set of variables and complexities. Several of the areas of greatest concern are as follows:

- **Legacy systems:** Large organizations have a portfolio of mission critical applications systems that can span multiple decades in their age and deployment. Organizations that have handled massive amounts of data for very long periods (like the federal government social security systems or the airline reservation system) may have technology that was created in the 1960's, and been brought forward and modified to connect to systems developed much later. Many of these systems were inspected and modified for the Y2K (Year 2000) switchover, but have not had significant security upgrades, and never anticipated being attached to a public network. In some cases, these systems cannot be changed easily or at all, either from a cost standpoint of a complete lack of personnel familiar with the complex inner workings and previous generation development environments.

- **Emerging technologies:** At the other end of the enterprise systems spectrum, new technologies are arriving at an astonishingly fast rate. Sensors, social media, mobile devices like smartphones and tablets have spawned an entirely new generation of internet and enterprise connected capabilities. Used for good, organizations can take advantage of state-of-the-art vehicles for communicating with the organization's customers and suppliers; generating instant information, analytics and actionable intelligence. Each of these emerging technologies enables the possibility of multiple attack vectors into the organization through the myriad of connections between the applications and devices and the organization's mission critical data. New technology opens the possibility of undetected errors in the software, or deliberate "backdoor" access for either maintenance or harm. Configuration errors such as not resetting the default password that comes with the technology may be another way that something new is exploited as an entry point into a well-established and otherwise security network.

- **Personal Devices:** BYOD (Bring your own Device) has been a major trend for the last several years as the IPHONE and IPAD have driven the desire to acquire cutting edge devices purchased with personal funds or expensed as office supplies. Inevitably, connecting for email access, file exchange and an array of other capabilities has been enabled, all in the name of increased productivity for the device owners. These devices can be fantastic – one client of mine took all his pre-sales materials and used a fleet of IPADS given to his manufacturer's reps as a great presentation tool that could be updated dynamically and eliminated significant printing expense. However, the reps started loading other manufacturer's sales information on the one device, despite the prohibition buried in the original company's usage agreement, enabling a cyber-vulnerability. If malicious code was picked up, the simple dissemination device could compromise the overall network – an unintended consequence in the design of the project.

- **Internal networks and facilities:** Inside the walls of an organization, things usually feel safer. There is usually some kind of access control system for letting people in, recognition by other staff members, and a general understanding of how things work. There can still be major security problems and attacks from many different access points. Access credentials that would never be written down in a coffee shop show up regularly on the bottom of keyboards or in a drawer. Memory sticks can carry a vast amount of information out the door in a pocket, or transport destructive malware into an otherwise secure network. Keyboard loggers can be inserted and capture sensitive information including passwords, enabling the theft of key credentials.

- **The Internet:** The Internet has become a fantastic resource for billions of people. On a personal note, the number of hours that I would have spent in a library 20 years ago researching this book would have dwarfed the time I gathered the information from hundreds of sources on the web. In addition, information can be published and updated in real time, shortening the time of creation to the time of consumption dramatically. The downside is that there are many possible attack vectors on people visiting sites and distributed denial of service (DDOS) attacks can greatly compromise an organization's network with large volumes of unwanted traffic.

- **Email:** Cyber security threats arrive in the mail every day through this vital communications channel. There might be an attachment that looks like it's from your shipping provider or your financial institution, but opening it can cause the beginnings of a cyber-attack. It may be a simple link that takes you to a site that you think is legitimate, but instead is an imitation site that collects your password to a legitimate site or downloads malicious software to your local computer. There has been good progress in automating controls of unsolicited emails, scanning for malware, and other activities in this area, but the threat persists through innovation and variation by the perpetrators. Many organizations are only one click away from a breach.

- **Physical infrastructure:** Physical infrastructure is increasingly controlled by computers and connected into the corporate network, which in turn is connected to the internet. This allows for vulnerabilities to be exploited, and puts an entire new threat into play. The Stuxnet computer worm was designed to find a very specific piece of hardware and disable a control, allowing a centrifuge to spin out of control and be damaged. If you have Industrial Control Systems (ICS), you are likely aware of these risks, but even simple systems like facility access control systems can be targeted, as well – what if someone could walk into your warehouse or research facility, ignoring all the automated security? All the perimeter security disappears if the invaders are in the building.

- **People:** People doing their jobs well are paramount in terms of preventing and mitigating attacks – and later in this book we'll focus on improving your direct and extended cyber teams. People issues are also cited in a large number of cyber situations as the cause or a supporting factor of many successful attacks. These people issues can be malicious, careless, or the result of completely inadvertent mistakes.

- How many passwords have you seen written down next to a keyboard over your career? How many security circumventions for existing systems are going on today in your organization? How many unauthorized devices are connected to your networks? When a malicious phishing email gets past your automated monitoring controls (if they are in place) and presented to 1,000 employees, do you have 100% confidence that nobody will inadvertently click on the link and immediately open the door for a malicious software download? People are paid to get things done, and security can be eased, forgotten, or completely circumvented in the pursuit of short term results.

Let's take a look at some of the astounding array of statistics published about organizations incurring cyber incidents and attacks. There are many information sources and many are listed in the later chapter on information resources. Every year brings newly summarized reports that are added to the general pool of knowledge about the cyber threat. This information is created by many diverse commercial, government and nonprofit groups, and can be difficult to correlate precisely. My recommendation is to find several sources that align well with your industry, and supplement them with paid subscription services to develop and maintain a good understanding and situational awareness of your specific risks.

These snippets should convince you that there is serious financial and reputational impact at stake for your organization:

The 2013 Ponemon Institute study found that the mean annualized cost for 60 benchmarked organizations is $11.6 million per year, with a range from $1.3 million to $58 million each year per company. 2012's mean cost per benchmarked organization was $8.9 million, resulting in a $2.6 million (26 percent) increased cost.

A 2012 Law and the Boardroom study found the average organizational loss from a data breach now exceeds $5.5 million, with U.S. businesses spending, on average, $8.9 million annually on cybercrime.

Following a significant data breach, TJX was sued by investors, forcing the parent of TJ Maxx and Marshall's to spend over $12 million in just one quarter on its breach response, legal, and other fees.

The Online Trust Alliance 2013 Data Protection & Breach Readiness Guide details that in 2012, 2,644 breaches were reported worldwide reflecting an increase of 117% over the 1,217 incidents reported in 2011. Combined, these incidents exposed over 267 million records. The largest reported breaches included Shanghai Roadway, Zappos and Global Payments, with 150, 26 and 7 million records exposed, respectively.

The following charts and graphs are a smattering of available information, and from the reports I found most useful in the research I've done in the production of this book. You will find that the numbers and methodologies vary widely, but the common theme is that the problem is enlarging, costs are spiraling, and there is little short-term hope for a reprieve from the relentless attacks happening against everyone from consumers to small business to multi-national business to foundations and governments worldwide. The statistics are staggering and clearly identify the cyber threat as a major risk area.

Average annualized cost by industry sector: (US $ millions)

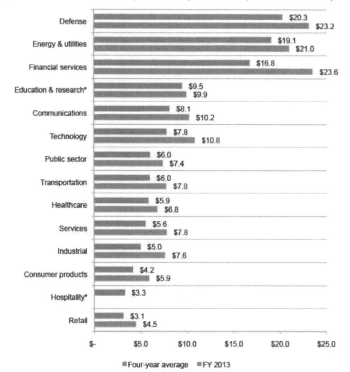

Source: Ponemon Institute 2013 Cost of Cyber Report

Average number of days to resolve attack type:

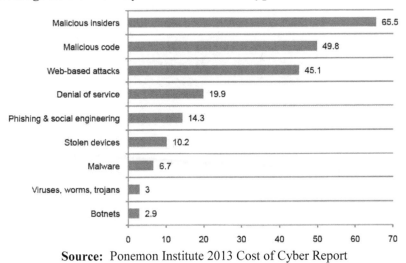

Malicious insiders — 65.5
Malicious code — 49.8
Web-based attacks — 45.1
Denial of service — 19.9
Phishing & social engineering — 14.3
Stolen devices — 10.2
Malware — 6.7
Viruses, worms, trojans — 3
Botnets — 2.9

Source: Ponemon Institute 2013 Cost of Cyber Report

This average number of days to resolve chart is very informative, showing that we are making progress on the more simplified attacks that have emerged over the years. Many organizations have installed high quality defense systems and there is an entire anti-virus and anti-malware industry that invests heavily in identifying new problems and distributing updates rapidly. The more complex attacks are much more difficult to unwind.

2012 International
Incident Highlights *

- 2,644 breaches (DDB)
- 26% from internal incidents
- 267 MM records (DDB)
- 94% server exploits (VZ)
- 97% avoidable (VZ)
- $194 cost @ record (SYMC)
- $5.5 MM cost @ breach (SYMC)
- $8.1 total billion costs (est)

SOURCE: OTA 2013 Data Protection & BreachReadiness Guide

The OTA study's metrics are another good point of reference and the item that stands out is the 97% avoidable statistic. With an increasing amount of information being categorized and shared publically and between organizations, a process where your organization can incorporate and rapidly analyze will bolster your defense.

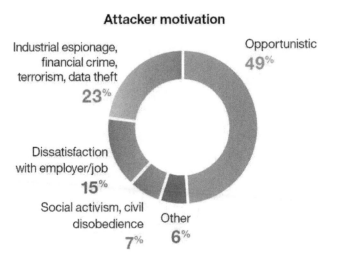

Source: IBM Security Services Cyber Security Intelligence Index

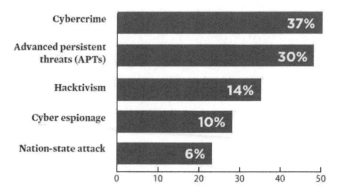

Source: FireEye: The Need for Speeed: 2013 Incident Response Survey

In the FireEye chart above, cyber criminals are the top concern for organizations polled in this study. These organizations are becoming increasingly sophisticated, as demonstrated by the attacks on Target and other retailers in the holiday season of 2013.

The area that is not addressed as a large concern is destruction of critical infrastructure like the electrical grid which indirectly could devestate many organizations.

What was the impact of the incident?

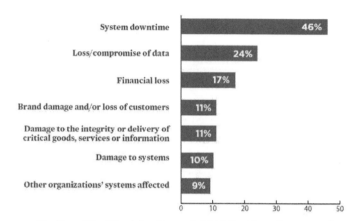

Source: FireEye: The Need for Speeed: 2013 Incident Response Survey

What do you identify as your greatest priority?

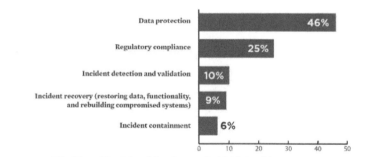

Source: FireEye: The Need for Speeed: 2013 Incident Response Survey

The cyber criminals are after sensitive and confidential data and the FireEye chart's respondents rightly identify this as a key area to protect. Losing information entrusted to you by your customers or intellectual property that cost millions or billions of dollars to produce is expensive and can kill an organization's reputation and relationship with customers.

There are many activities that your organization can initiate in order to prepare and mitigate your crititical data from simple attacks, and a growing arsenal of products and services that will help identify serious attacks.

Chapter 1 Key Points Summary:

The cyber security threat has grown significantly in the last 10 years, with new attacks appearing on a continual and unrelenting basis. No organization has been immune from attack.

The costs of a sweeping, successful attack can be enormous – monetary, reputational, operational, morale, long-term intellectual property and more. These costs can be immediate and continue to impact your bottom line for years.

Attacks can come from different groups of attackers and target different aspects of your information technology systems.

There are many ways to assess the threat, but the evolving nature of this area does not allow an easy quantification of the risk and the cost of complete avoidance.

Our use of computing has grown exponentially over the last 30 years and permeated every aspect of our organizations. With the widespread adoption of cloud computing and the Internet of Things (IOT), this usage trend will accelerate rather than stabilize, expanding the cyber security risk surface.

Personal devices extend productivity, but can be a conduit for attackers leading into an organization's key computing resources.

Everyone in the organization must be involved in defense – this is not an isolated IT problem.

Chapter 2: Cyber - Not Your Everyday Risk!

"As the United States attorney in Manhattan, I have come to worry about few things as much as the gathering cyber threat." - Preet Bharara

Organizations have been dealing with group risk since the formation of the earliest groups in civilization – tribes, clans and bands.   Individual risks abounded for every unique man, woman and child on the planet.   Then, a rustling in the bushes could be friend or foe. Today, we have an intuitive sense of risk when we drive, fly, or participate in any number of everyday activities – the fight or flight instinct has persisted in our genetic makeup.   The risk of a cyber-attack is new within our lifetime and civilization is still grasping to understand the threat and its relative impact.

What is risk?   We all use the term "risk" freely in our personal and business lives, but if you put a group of people on the spot to define it clearly, it's a difficult concept to quantify.   One concise definition from the dictionary is "a situation involving exposure to danger."   Two other good summary definitions are "possibility of loss or injury" and "someone or something that creates or suggests a hazard."   Cyber security issues fit all of these definitions and qualify for some descriptive adjectives like "unbounded" and "non-quantifiable" risks. Unlike other risks, it is very difficult today to completely understand the full damage that could be done by the broad set of threats available to cyber attackers.

Corporations and other large organizations have done a commendable job of managing most risks through insurance, contingency planning, exercises and an array of other methods to prepare, prevent, mitigate and recover from a wide variety of impactful situations – acts of man; acts of nature; criminal acts; acts of stupidity. On the positive side of risk, many corporations owe their existence to taking a risk: on a new product, a new market, or an aggressive campaign against competitors. We're a risk-based society and each of us has a difference tolerance.

In recent years, many large organizations have formalized risk planning through the creation of the Chief Risk Officer and an organization-wide risk management planning approach. The Chief Risk Officer has access to the many guidelines set out in the multiple Enterprise Risk Management (ERM) frameworks that have emerged as this activity has become more codified. There are large groups of consultants who assist organizations in the ERM planning and execution. Risk assessment is an important component in major decisions made by large organizations. Boards of directors will frequently examine the risk points for the organization they are tasked with guiding, working to anticipate and minimize possible disruption. Determining the right amount of risk is an important element of an organization's overall strategy.

Cyber security risks have many similar elements to the existing risk portfolio being dealt with by organizations worldwide, and we'll review many of the standard processes that can be applied from an enterprise risk management framework later in this book. **Cyber security risks have some unique characteristics that set**

it apart as a unique element that can impact the very existence of the organization. Contrary to many enterprise risk management conventions, I don't recommend treating the cyber threat as a normal type of risk; until there is some stabilization, there are too many variables and unknowns. It is important to isolate the area of cyber threats and treat it as a unique, dangerous risk for your organization.

Anecdote - Fire in Medieval Cities: Fire was a major natural force for mankind to harness and spawned untold capabilities and uses throughout its long tenure in our civilization's development. Today, we certainly plan for fire safety, as there seems to have been an increase in large scale wildfires attributed to global warming. However, we don't treat fire as crippling risk that can eliminate our organizations – the risk has been handled, codified, and largely automated except for the worst circumstances. That wasn't always the case, however. In the era of the medieval city, fire had many of the same risk elements as cyber threats today:

- **Overgrown, rapid growth:** Cities experienced rapid growth, many times unconstrained by planning, zoning or future thinking. The mission was more commerce - more people, more factories – very similar to today's rapid spread of technology in the name of productivity gains and competitive advantage. The opportunity and the risk went hand in hand.

- **Malicious or inadvertent starting points**: Major fires could be started as easily as a cow kicking over a candle or as malicious as an arsonist with an oil-soaked torch setting strategic points ablaze. Once the incident was underway, it was often too late to prevent widespread destruction. A culture of risk awareness and continual vigilance had to be maintained, but could be circumvented easily by anyone; including children and intoxicated adults. It's a wonder there weren't many more devastating fires under these circumstances.

- **Inter-connections:** As houses and structures grew, they became closer and more linked together, increasing population density, but allowing a fast interconnection for spread of fire. Few or no physical firewalls existed

- **Primitive materials**: Most structures were made of wood which could easily propagate a fire to other areas away from the origin making it very hard to contain an incident.

- **No automated defenses**: Since electricity had yet to be invented, smoke detectors, sprinkler systems and fire alarms were out of the question.

Until we address some of the key historical problems around cyber security and the technology that we work with today, cyber security demands an elevated level of attention and is distinctly different from all other risks your organization faces for a number of reasons:

Massive impact potential: Cyber-attacks can be the organizational equivalent of a large meteor hitting Earth – even with all of our advanced technology, we could be blindsided and have a massive impact happen with almost no notice. The worse news is that the probability of a devastating cyber event in your organization is much higher than the planet and meteor collision scenario. While not all cyber-attacks create a massive level of damage, your organization needs to be cognizant of how bad things could be in the worst case scenario, preparing accordingly. You could also be indirectly affected – a regional attack on the power grid could cripple your organization if it is located in the impact zone. Numerous pundits have predicted a sustained power outage in a region where a devastating cyber-attack disables the electrical grid, plunging all geographically located organizations into total darkness for months while critical equipment is sourced and replaced.

Long-term damage: Long after the initial recovery has taken place, certain cyber incidents can have a major impact on your reputation as a company. If your customer records were breached and millions of people were inconvenienced by having to get new credit cards or reset their passwords, you can bet the memory of that experience will last a significant amount of time.

Real time nature: Cyber events can happen in real time or sneak up on you over months or years – intruders may be inside your network at this very moment. Detection can be very difficult depending on the nature and speed of the threat. Once detected, however, your organization will need a real time response to mitigate the damage already caused or being caused. Seconds can be important to your response, and as automated defenses continue to improve, micro-seconds will come into play on both the attack side and defense side. This real time response is not just for the IT-managed data center. You will have multiple areas of the organization impacted that will need the same rapid response, potentially all the way up the board helping to mitigate brand damage with the media.

Global reach: Conventional risk wisdom has been that "all disasters are local," but the cyber threat defies this previously sage advice. A cyber-attack can impact your organization in every corner of the globe at the same moment in time with no warning. When the Sony PlayStation network was compromised around April 2011, the attack had an immediate impact on multiple continents and the entire global organization. While geographic incidents can be devastating – like the 2004 Christmas time tsunami in Indonesia or the Japanese earthquake/tsunami in March 2011 – the impacts are ultimately localized, and steps can be taken to shift requirements, production, personnel and other key elements to an area unaffected by the incident. Major cyber-attacks can cut to the core across an organization's global presence, impacting every point on the planet in an instant. The same technology suite that allows for lightning fast communications, worldwide customer reach, financial consolidations and other key global functions can be turned against an organization that is globally positioned.

Difficulty in assessment: While some attacks are easy to understand, detect, and respond to, many are very difficult to immediately understand, and may have multiple attack elements. As an example, let's suppose your CFO leaves his personal iPad in the back of an American Airlines seat pocket when his flight lands in Cleveland. The iPad is returned eight hours later after some frantic phone calls by his administrative assistant – whew! However, what is unknown to all is that someone scanned and copied the stored data on the device during the lost and found time, and sold that information to someone who understands how to look for passwords, sensitive documents, and other long-term compromise points. Is there any damage? If so, how bad is the impact? When will it manifest itself? If the CFO is using his personal device, has it been protected or audited by internal IT security staff to insure some level of protection is available? What if nobody realizes there was a compromise for 6-9 months? What damage could be done during that timeframe if the wrong information had been unprotected, and its continual use undetected? Could the information theft set up both a personal and corporate attack?

Many attack vectors: Your organization can be attacked in many different places – inside and outside the organization. The widespread, and many times uncoordinated, use of information technology lends itself to this and a map of all the connections, devices, applications, and data flows within your organization will give you a good sense of this – if you can construct one at all. Employees working at home, in the field, or telecommuting from home widen your exposure greatly, as do live network connections to key suppliers and customers. Physical access and theft of actual devices can also constitute a major threat.

Many attack sources: The bad guys looking to inflict harm on your organization can be very different in nature. In some of the worst situations, nation-states can be attacking in an effort to get long term strategic documents and plans, as noted in attacks against the Department of Defense and Lockheed Martin. While no war resulted, damage was definitely assessed and much diplomatic finger-pointing ensued. Organized crime has a big incentive toward cyber-crimes – the risk of getting caught is lower and the likely monetary gains are higher. Attacks can take place across borders, further complicating the jurisdictional elements and making prosecution harder. We've also seen groups of "hacktivists" that disrupt technology capabilities for reasons cited as more altruistic – the United States had to bear the impact of Bradley Manning stealing hundreds of thousands of classified messages and documents and releasing them through WikiLeaks is a good example of this

Insider threat: One of the worse cyber scenarios you can encounter is a malicious insider. Regardless of whether you view

Edward Snowden as a legitimate whistle-blower or a villainous traitor, there is little discussion to be had about the way he obtained all the information he spirited away to international locations: he used his legitimately-issued Top Secret credentials to log in and copy information outside of the authorized systems. This occurred in what is reportedly one of the most secure computing environments in the world – so what damage could an empowered, high level, disgruntled employee do to your internal organizational systems?

Targeting: There are many garden variety cyber-attacks that your organization is subject to without any differentiation by the attackers – one organization is the same as any other. They happen every day, and many of the best intrusion detection and vulnerability detection systems will do a credible job of preventing them. An area for specific board attention is a targeted, coordinated attack that is aimed at the heart of your organization. In a targeted attack, you could be dealing with an entity that will utilize multiple attack vectors against you and have a very specific target in mind – for example, intellectual property that will be your organization's lifeline for the next 20 years – drug designs, airplane schematics, source code and many more things that have moved from physical to digital in the last 25 years. Imagine the multiple ways your organization could be attacked through your global network, your suppliers, bribing your people, injecting malware, physically breaching your security and copying information directly. Those are just a few of the ways a highly coordinated attack could play out over a number of months or years.

What do I win if my organization does everything right? When you are doing everything right, you get to keep on surviving as an organization. You don't get a direct return to your bottom line and you don't ever get to a point where you can become complacent and relaxed – the barbarians are at the gate waiting for a slip. Survival is the prize, sad to say. This continual cost of doing business is troublesome to many executive leadership teams and, when other areas of the business demand more dollars, can lead to skimping or budget reductions in the day to day or long term cyber defenses. In the long run, if all organizations work together, this problem may become more routine and manageable, but we are far from that point in 2014.

The case for a nation versus nation cyber war: There have been numerous books and articles on the topic of cyber war, and the *New York Times* ran a compelling series of articles about the possibilities in 2010. No formal cyber war has been declared and fought by sovereign nations in my unclassified research. There have definitely been skirmishes and incidents; with many not disclosed to the general public. Despite my living in the Washington, DC area, I have no intimate or classified knowledge into the Intelligence Community or State Department or Department of Defense on this topic. My working opinion is that no serious war in the near future would only be cyber based – I think the side losing the confrontation would certainly deploy traditional, kinetic attacks in a desperate attempt to shift the balance of the engagement if they started losing the cyber confrontation. I also can't imagine a traditional war that didn't involve cyber-attacks on the other side.

The case for a large scale terrorist cyber-attack: This situation is one from the movies – one bad guy suddenly controls the entire United States computer resources. He or she can crash a plane on demand, turn out the lights in a major city, or wipe out trillions in wealth at a major financial institution. Pay the ransom or let the other terrorists out of prison if you ever want to see your data or critical infrastructure again.

Is this feasible in today's technological world? Opinions would vary greatly in terms of what could be possible, and likely scenarios would be a subset of those possibilities. My focus in this book is on the individual organization and how they can work to keep themselves protected and share information synergistically with others. I am most worried about regional attacks that could disrupt critical infrastructure like power or communications. The U.S. federal government and other governments around the world are continually monitoring these possibilities.

Fighting like the underdog: I just finished reading the audiobook version of Malcolm Gladwell's *David and Goliath: Underdogs, Misfits, and the Art of Battling Giants*. In the book, Gladwell talks about several battles where the underdogs surprised the established leaders and won the day's victory. One story stood out to me: the efforts of Viveck Ranadive and the coaching of his 12-year-old daughter's basketball team. Ranadive had never played or coached basketball; he was the founder of a software company. The team had much less going for it compared to its opponents, but won an amazing number of games through their use of the full court press, panicking the opposition into throwing the ball away or turning it over, and playing defense the entire length of the court. Ranadive was quoted as saying "all the other team had to do to beat us was

38

give us a taste of our own medicine in order to beat us, because we couldn't take that pressure either."

A similar comparison can be made to our cyber defenses - we need to have our organizations maintain a continual defensive effort on our unseen opponents, scratching for every advantage, and sharing those hard fought lessons with other organizations fighting the same attackers. With an immense attack surface to defend, it's the large established organizations that are the underdogs in this battle. Everyone should work to put the full court press on the attackers.

Chapter 2 Key Points Summary:

Cyber is a unique risk for the organization, and should **_not_** be lumped into the normal pool of potential risks faced by your organization.

Many vendors are mobilizing solutions to solve different parts of the problem, but an overall risk picture defies definition because of the rapid changes and undiscovered vulnerabilities.

Every large enterprise system is a unique combination of applications and components, defying completely standardized defenses.

The impact of a cyber-security incident can range from silent and undetected to devastating and immediate.

Damages from a cyber-attack can be short term and/or long term with many variations and permutations.

There is no standard, analytical risk model for calculating the odds or impact of a successful attack or the right amount to spend on defenses.

Innovation on the perpetrator's part is advancing rapidly, and information sharing between the bad guys happening continually through the open web and private communications.

Resilience is an attitude that must be incorporated into action so that one cyber torpedo does not scuttle the entire organizational aircraft carrier.

Everyone in the organization must be involved in cyber defense – this is not an isolated IT problem.

Chapter 3: Leadership – Board and Executive Issues

"...Hope is not a strategy." - Rudy Giuliani

Executive and board leadership on cyber security issues are critical and necessary to an organization's chances of long term survival of today's cyber threats. As described in the previous chapter, the risks are critical and a major impact on your organization could be encountered at any moment in time. The board of directors must set the direction and parameters for the company and work to insure that this strategic direction is being carefully deployed through the executive team inside the entire organization.

Bigger than an IT issue: Too many organizations think that cyber threat preparation and response is an IT issue and best left to the technical people in the organization. This is short-sighted thinking and will cause you immense pain if don't widen your thought process to the entire organization. The board and executive leadership should understand the complexities of legal, regulatory, customer and many other issues that transcend the IT component of information security and incident response. Being proactive and involving the entire organization into the preparation process will be critical, and in many cases, an executive other than the CIO or CISO will be required to lead the response to a major breach or incident.

Being technical: One of the most cited reasons for directors and senior executive's failure to adequately understand and apply governance and oversight for cyber security issues (and enterprise information technology, in general) is that the directors are older and don't understand technology. While the data confirms that most directors are in their sixties and seventies, and don't have degrees in computer science or information technology, I think it is a complete abdication of responsibility to use a lack of understanding as an excuse for inaction or non-involvement on the cyber threat.

The world is a complex place and all directors have a lifetime of experience of dealing with ambiguity of many types. Most directors have risen from the ranks through their intelligence, adaptability, and persistence across a wide range of industries. The idea that the essence of the cyber security problem can't be comprehended or given proper oversight by the board or senior executive team members is a non-starter for me, and would extrapolate that to litigation around attacks. Imagine an attorney quizzing a board member, "you oversaw the multi-billion dollar merger of two global corporations with 22 product lines and operating in 48 countries, but you couldn't figure out how to direct your IT staff to protect critical data?" The board has the power and obligation to demand explanations and recommended action in the language of business and risk. The board must exercise this prerogative to do their fiduciary duty.

I would agree that most board members will have no value added when it comes to picking between two competing intrusion detection systems that operate inside the organization's worldwide TCP/IP network and shouldn't be involved with the detail of those decisions. However, understanding industry comparable information on attacks, insuring the right people are hired and paying attention to the oversight details, and setting the "tone from the top" on cyber risk awareness all fall into the purview of the board, and we'll discuss many relevant issues that do not rely on technological depth. The board must exert a great deal of leadership in the face of imperfect information on threats, solutions, risks and courses of action.

Avoiding personal liability: If you are a corporate director, there are definite risks associated with cyber security. This is an area that can strip an organization of its intellectual property and reputation in minutes. I am not a lawyer and have no basis for advising you on the laws around negligence and other areas that can be brought to bear through litigation. There are some excellent documents available on the web by capable law firms that address these issues and I've listed several in the resource section. My non-legal advice is to be highly pro-active around this topic and drive your organization to a very solid set of defensive capabilities administered by topnotch people. Doing nothing is a recipe for disaster on several fronts.

I recently attended the Annual Conference for the National Association of Corporate Directors (www.nacdonline.org) and was a speaker on a breakout panel focused on the cyber risk facing today's corporations and nonprofits. Attendance was high and interest very enthusiastic toward understanding the board's role in this emerging cyber landscape. We had an intense discussion on policy, tactics, strategy, government, people and future directions. At a break, one director confidentially described the helplessness the board felt when they had to shut down their critical business systems for two weeks due to a major breach from sophisticated perpetrators – the impact was significant and they hadn't been prepared to respond. It cost them some money, but hurt their reputation much more. She vowed to be more prepared in the future.

Best Management Practice	Regularly	Occasionally	Rarely or Never
Board reviews & approves top-level policies on privacy & IT security risks	23%	28%	42%
Board reviews & approves roles & responsibilities of lead personnel responsible for privacy & IT security	19%	18%	66%
Board reviews & approves annual budgets for privacy & IT security programs	28%	10%	54%
Board regularly receives reports from senior mgmt regarding privacy & IT security risks	38%	34%	25%

Source: Carnegie Mellon CYLAB 2012 report on enterprise security

The CYLAB report snippet reference above illustrates that improvement on cyber awareness is sorely needed at the board of director's levels. These figures represent poor oversight for a risk that can scuttle the entire organization. One non-cyber event to keep in mind as an example is the Costa Concordia cruise ship – in January 2012, a $2 billion asset was converted into a gigantic liability in an instant of negligence or bad luck; the captain was off course and hit a rock that sank the ship and killed multiple people. Did the board of that organization do everything possible there to hire and vet the captain responsible for this $2 billion plus insurance loss? If your organization falls victim to a devastating breach of security, will you be able to justify to your stakeholders (and their attorneys) that you did all that was reasonably possible?

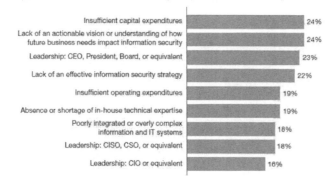

Figure 13: Greatest obstacles to improving information security

Obstacle	Percentage
Insufficient capital expenditures	24%
Lack of an actionable vision or understanding of how future business needs impact information security	24%
Leadership: CEO, President, Board, or equivalent	23%
Lack of an effective information security strategy	22%
Insufficient operating expenditures	19%
Absence or shortage of in-house technical expertise	19%
Poorly integrated or overly complex information and IT systems	18%
Leadership: CISO, CSO, or equivalent	18%
Leadership: CIO or equivalent	16%

Note: Totals do not add up to 100%. Respondents were allowed to indicate multiple factors.

SOURCE: PWC Defending Yesterday, Key findings from The Global State of Information Security® Survey 2014

The previous PWC report graph is not cyber specific, but information security is a broader category that has a strong effect on cyber defense. The top four categories support the importance and need to improve board oversight – capital expenditures are a function of leadership and strategy.

A lesson from the past: To counter an invasion threat, the French built an impressive set of interlocking fortresses across the border with Germany known as the Maginot Line. In World War I, the defenses served the country well. In World War II, the Germans completely circumvented these impressive defenses by using a blitzkrieg ("Lightning War"), driving around the defensive line through the Netherlands and Benelux countries. The lesson learned was that as capabilities changed, certain defenses were no longer relevant and needed to be updated no matter how impressive they seemed. Insure your organization is not caught short with only technologies and defenses from the cyber vulnerabilities of five years ago. This is an evolving battle and the weapons are changing frequently.

Several key areas where the board and executive leadership team are especially important:

Encouraging honest assessment and feedback: I've been listening to many reviews of what went wrong with the U.S. government's www.healthcare.gov launch from a technical standpoint. The most relevant part to our discussion has been the apparent shielding of President Obama and Health and Human Service Secretary Katherine Sibelius from the facts that the web site wasn't ready for prime time usage as the promised implementation date grew near. Many people apparently knew or had predicted the debacle long before the grim reality arrived. If you are feeling pretty good about your cyber security strategy and implementation, you might want to insure that you are getting treated honestly by your experts, and not being shielded from the hard truths in this critical area. It is very difficult to deliver bad news to the board and senior executives of an organization. You are going to have to work hard to insure you are fully in the loop while the guidance you can provide will still be on the proactive side. Finding out after the fact is very painful.

Governance and oversight: This is the board's central purpose – I've heard it summarized as "nose in, fingers out" implying full understanding and strategic direction without micromanaging. For the cyber threat, a comprehensive overview of the organization is required and the board should be tasked with working through this issue with the full management team. The board should communicate across the organization how this oversight is accomplished, enabling individuals at all levels to contribute innovative ideas and flag potential problems before they reach massive proportions.

Hiring and development of the cyber team: In my opinion, this is the single crucial area where more efforts can return a high rate of return on time invested. The board and the senior executive team are going to rely on the people and organizations that are put into place to manage, operate and defend the organization on a 24/7 basis. Many boards make the mistake in isolating these efforts to the Information Technology group inside their organization and not casting a wider net across the entire company. The effective team will almost always be cross functional, cutting across departmental barriers and information silos, and embracing the cyber threat as the multi-headed beast that it really is. In the IT world, great people are in great demand and there aren't enough good people either. You need to insure your people are the best you can get, verifying at the beginning with comprehensive background checks, periodic re-evaluations, and verification of their capabilities through the use of outside (and thoroughly vetted) experts that can give you a full appraisal of competence and readiness.

Prioritization: Every organization has areas that are significantly more important than others, and the board and executive leadership team are best situated to identify these critical areas. Once identified, special care should be taken in the protection and response to these areas. For example, a drug company may have extremely sensitive research and development systems that if compromised, could cost the organization billions of dollars in later revenue through intellectual property theft. Similarly, banks have millions of customer records that demand enhanced protection measures. Insuring that the leadership of the organization has clearly communicated the priorities and is aggressively following up with the operational functions is a great first step in the protection of these invaluable assets. Some industry solutions may be prohibitively expensive if applied to all the information technology throughout the organization, but perfectly rational and affordable for those specific, important areas identified.

Balance: The cyber security problem we're examining is severe, immediate, and very dangerous – make no mistake. In my opinion you should take a committed approach toward these preparation and assessment efforts. In every other organization, there are dozens of other key opportunities and problems that demand attention and activity by the board and senior management. There is little point of having a five year cyber security initiative if you are losing money and heading for bankruptcy in eight weeks! The example is a little extreme, but cash flow, sales, product planning, succession planning and a myriad of other items will demand the board's attention in any given reporting period. Building the base of education and understanding around cyber, and having the flexibility to allocate additional leadership resources in the event of a major shortfall is also an important element of balancing all these different items.

Culture of risk awareness: As previously discussed, almost anyone in the organization can be an entry point for a cyber-attack, either maliciously or inadvertently. In most organizations, the information technology team is very risk aware and tries to sensitize everyone to the risks associated with poor cyber hygiene.

In many of the same organizations, IT is looked upon as impediment to progress rather than the fount of wisdom on all things technology. The same risk message coming from the board will have a different voice. Bill Gates, as Chairman of Microsoft in his Trustworthy Computing memo of January 15, 2002 set the challenge for the entire company that resulted in a quantitative shift toward security awareness internally and in the product development groups. Like so many companies today, Microsoft must protect its own information and systems, but also is one of the world's biggest providers of software and information services. Board leadership in your organization is an important element to your overall strategy for reducing risk. The board and executive leadership can sensitize and make everyone aware of the risks and impact of a major cyber incident.

Strategic Budgeting: Allocating dollars in a way that balances the organization's needs is a daunting task, even in the best of times. The complexities of short term and long term spending, impact on the bottom line, risk management and the ability to adapt to changing circumstances is challenging for all boards even in areas that are well understood. How do you budget for the right amount of spending for a threat that is largely undefined, multi-faceted, and changing very quickly? How do you allocate dollars to all areas of the organization where planning and preparation have to take place? How do you insure that dollars allocated and spent are synergistic across the organization and effective in their results? The answer comes back around to the discussion of hiring top-notch individuals and validating their efforts through outside expertise.

Collaboration inside the silos: Sad to say, but factions, silos, and fiefdoms exist within most large organizations. The board and the executive team are responsible for making these different factions work together proactively in the defense of the organization from cyber-attacks. For example, the Chief Security Officer might have a full command center for monitoring the physical parts of the organizations – fences, access doors, high value areas and others. This command center should be able to reposition its efforts in an emergency and assist in the incident response called for by a cyber-attack. Many of the same alerting systems should be common to the physical and cyber response organizations so that personnel inside the organization have less to remember between incidents. By combining your efforts and resources, you should realize a better result.

Outside verification: No matter how good your internal people are it is next to impossible to stay up to date completely and have a totally objective view of your cyber policies, controls, defenses, response and future directions. Getting an independent resource to assess and verify these critical areas is a powerful cross-check that should not be skipped or skimped on. Using an outsider can also create a trail of documentation that will outlast generations of employees, serve as a good reminder of what was important in given time periods, and what was distributed and discussed inside the leadership team. There may need to be multiple outside groups involved with this process. NOTE: this is not a blanket endorsement for legions of consultants taking up residence in your organization for years on end. Finding the right groups who can help you on an as-needed basis and be available to surge into action in the event of an incident is likely a more rational strategy.

Real time response: The board needs to set the stage for a real time response to an incident that could impact the future of the organization. Planning and preparation must be coordinated, scenarios validated, contingency agreements executed, and outside verification obtained – all supported by exercises to reinforce activities and look for gaps in the planning. There is an old adage that may be helpful: "failing to plan is planning to fail." This kind of rehearsal time is always difficult to schedule, execute thoroughly, and make inclusive to everyone that needs the critical understanding and preparation for the real event. Cyril Richard "Rick" Rescorla (May 27, 1939 – September 11, 2001), security director for Morgan Stanley in New York's World Trade Center was known for being persistent and dogmatic about preparedness and evacuation drills and exercises – even with high level executives. He is credited with saving a large number of lives in the 9/11 attacks, and lost his own life evacuating more personnel from the South Tower. Training and preparation paid off for the individuals he impacted at Morgan Stanley, and sets a profound example for all of us. Apply the same efforts in your organization and you'll reap the benefits.

Compliance: Many industries will have very specific compliance requirements generated by the nature of their activities and historical legislation and regulation. Compliance is often thought of as a reporting task, minimizing the underlying work that results in a satisfactory rating on the paperwork. Utilizing the knowledge gained long after the compliance paperwork has been submitted is important for the organization. Oversight to insure that the compliance efforts are being incorporated into the organization is a key metric for a successful program.

Audit: The audit committee of the board of directors is typically charged with monitoring risk management activities. The committee is a subset of the board of directors and reports into the board. Some boards are establishing separate technical oversight committees as the breadth of technology continues to broaden. Whatever way your particular organization does it, having a strong audit function around cyber threats and preparedness is an important oversight element. Metrics are important to gather on an ongoing basis in order to assess the success or failure of your cyber efforts. If an attack happens, a good understanding of what went wrong and corrective measures is imperative.

Information sharing: As I will cover in a later chapter, information sharing is an important defense that should be utilized to improve your situational awareness. Because most directors are on multiple boards, there are some high level sharing discussions that can take place between board members in terms of threats, preparation, exercises, response and recovery. I would encourage you to pursue as many of these as possible – the enhanced knowledge will help all concerned. If necessary, you can complete non-disclosure agreements to keep the information more confidential, or ask for non-attribution when the information isn't already identifiable to your organization. The board and executive team should also understand and promote multiple sharing efforts with the government, consortiums, industry groups, and partners to help build a more comprehensive set of defenses and awareness.

Future: The world changes quickly and it seems like the pace has continued to accelerate despite the worldwide economic slowdown that has plagued many organizations for the last five or more years. The executive leadership of the organization has to be thinking about the future, both from a new opportunity and expansion footing, and from a risk awareness element. How will the new wireless product line be impacted by security? Have we built defenses into the product, or will we be forced to modify the technology on the fly as hackers probe every digital orifice available, maybe some we don't even know about? Is the new enterprise resource management going to help or hurt us from a security standpoint? Our suppliers are demanding real time access to information; can we accomplish the competitive goal without compromising our overall corporate exposure? Will the new cloud computing initiative allow us to segregate our information and will the vendor be better or worse than our internal people at protecting it? I have added a full chapter about future implications in the cyber world toward the end of this book and would encourage you to create a detailed roadmap of the issues coming toward you – looking at how they could improve your organization, but also at any new threats created by their adoption.

Board makeup and structure: Several of the board members I interviewed mentioned that they had specifically recruited members who were much more technically aware to insure that the board had an enhanced strategic awareness of the organization's activities around cyber and information management. Several had created a technical sub-committee who were responsible for more detailed drill down into these areas, and then briefing the entire board. I'm not a board structure/governance expert, but this approach rings true to me as a method for more scrutiny and oversight of these issues. One of the best groups I've encountered for guidance on these types of issues is the National Association of Corporate Directors (www.nacdonline.org).

Chapter 3 Key Points Summary:

The Board of Directors has final responsibility and oversight to an organization's planning and response to cyber threats.

"Hope is not a strategy" – you need to be proactive and decisive on the cyber threats long before dealing with an attack or breach.

The board and executive team must insure that they are getting honest, direct information on cyber efforts. Being lulled into complacency or treated like a mushroom is a recipe for disaster.

The board and executive team has to insist on strategy and plans presented in a way that can be understood, not shrouded in tech-speak. Insist on a translation, or bring someone in from the outside who can help accomplish this vital communications effort.

The board has to help hire and validate the right people inside the organization to monitor and respond to cyber threats. This extends beyond the information technology group. Extra diligence, background checks, outside validation and continual verification are recommended.

The board has to create a "tone at the top" for cyber risk awareness, making the entire organization aware and vigilant.

Get outside verification and validation on your people, plans, processes and preparation. There are many good organizations that can provide a cross-check on your efforts.

The board and executive team have to prioritize and allocate sufficient budget for cyber protection efforts. Cutting corners on spending can quickly become a short-sighted saving.

The board has to insure that there is a cross-organizational team, planning, exercises and response. Leaving the entire problem in the hands of the Information Technology department is a mistake, no matter how capable they are technically or operationally.

The board has to insure that the cyber security issue is being addressed across the company – this is not an isolated IT problem.

Chapter 4: Cyber Intelligence – Preparing and Prevention

"An ounce of prevention is worth a pound of cure" - Benjamin Franklin

Situation: Visualize that today is a day like most others. Business is proceeding apace within your global organization and all things seem normal. Information is flowing, customers are being interacted with, research is being conducted along with innumerable other functions across 78 countries around the world. Business is operating 24/7, with the sun never setting on your efforts to dominate your chosen markets. Life is good, or at least, it doesn't suck.

Who, at this very moment, is consumed and obsessed with keeping things on an even keel and preparing for the almost inevitable moment when the organization must react to a massively threatening situation? Who is thinking about the different groups trying to take advantage of your most important information – customers, intellectual property, physical control systems, and financial accounts? Who is standing watch?

The Ben Franklin quote at the start of this chapter is as applicable today as it was in the 1700's. Putting the right preparedness steps into place is the best use of your time and resources. You might not avoid all attacks, but a disciplined proactive approach will help even if you need to move into incident response mode and handle a major breach.

There are many elements to the proper preparation and prevention activities that have to be carried out in order to keep a vigilant watch out for major incidents or the first steps of an intruder creeping toward creating a major data breach. While some automated defenses are moving into mainstream use, most of the many activities you can do to prepare have people associated with them– configuration, monitoring, analytics, alarms and alerts that need to be handled by internal resources or by very well vetted outside service providers.

Who is leading the cyber defense team? The CEO is ultimately responsible for the activities of the organization, but rarely is he or she the operational leader for your cyber security efforts. In many organizations, the Chief Information Security Officer (CISO) or Chief Information Officer (CIO) is the person responsible for standing watch and managing the day to day efforts across the organization. It is important that there is a cross-departmental approach and that the team leader is working to inform and communicate with all segments of the organization. In addition, the overall team leader has to manage upward and outward as well as down into the organization – keeping senior executives and the board informed and primed to execute their roles in the event of an emergency. The outward focus is on information sharing and community, understanding best practices in your given industry or the cyber world at large. The leader of your efforts is a critical position.

Depending on the industry, capitalization (public or private company), organizational size, structure (full hierarchy versus independent divisions) and numerous other factors, the internal structure of your cyber efforts will vary in terms of reporting, responsibility and response. Critical to the structure is building a team that is not hamstrung by politics or lengthy approval procedures, and has a direct notification and ability to act built into its charter. The team should be cross functional, and understand the entire scope of the organization's operations. When urgency is called for, the team should have access to the key management necessary to make decisions.

Who is on the direct team? Who is dedicated to the cyber security mission on a continual basis? The answer to this question will help assess how serious the organization is to preventing problems and to building a response capability. Obviously, there is a major difference between the resources and risks run by a local chair manufacturer, a regional electrical utility and a global bank, but it is vital to understand which elements are well-considered differences versus just made by default. If the attackers are committed full time to gaining access to your information resources, and your response toward prevention is a part time resource allocation, you may be tipping the long term scales in favor of the intruders. There are many aspects of the direct team activities that should be considered:

- Is there continual attention/monitoring 24/7/365 of network and system metrics?

- Are there real people watching or are you using remote alerting from monitoring applications?

- Is threat monitoring and prevention a full time job or a part time effort?

- Are there written procedures for notification and escalation if something happens?

- Is there a coordinated, integrated effort between the organization's physical security efforts and the information security efforts?

- What kind of training has the dedicated team received? Technical training is imperative, but training in communications and incident response in the event of an immediate emergency is also recommended.

- Are there organizational resources who can monitor the customer experience from the outside, detecting attacks that only outsiders can view?

What does your extended team look like? The makeup of the direct team usually includes insiders, both employees and service providers, who are fully or partially dedicated to cyber defenses. Extended teams encompass employees and outside resources that can be mobilized in the event of a heightened sense of risk that is triggered by either outside intelligence, internal monitoring, or some other advance notification that identifies an upcoming problem. If you think about the volunteer fire departments that have been and are still prevalent across the United States, you get a good idea of how a set of volunteers can be mobilized in the event of a threat, having trained ahead of time to ensure the right response. In the world of large organizations, "surge" resources that can be brought to bear when required rather than being always available are becoming a very good way to save budget for actual incident response.

This does not mean picking up the phone book and trying to engage a random resource when something terrible happens – it presumes a rational engagement set up ahead to time with known costs, service level agreements, and any necessary training/exercises necessary to ensure a coordinated result when the situation demands it. Knowing who is going to be on your extended team in an emergency is an important factor toward a good response. Proactive coordination is a key preparedness activity.

Security anecdote: I worked with one of the most recognized and comprehensive private security companies for 18 months as an innovation consultant. They handled a wide range of security issues on a continual and pre-contracted emergency basis – executive protection, event security, internal investigations and fraud prevention. I was in the car with the Washington DC manager when he got a call from a company who wanted "an agent with a gun" because one of the operations people had muttered that he was going home at lunch to get his Glock handgun and eliminate the marketing department over some kind of dispute. The security manager carefully pointed the prospective customer toward the police because trying to establish a contractual relationship under these circumstances was almost impossible. A little bit of pre-planning would have gone a long way toward resolving this problem for the organization - establishing contingent resources is an important element of pre-planning for emergency incident response.

The extended team is typically more cross-functional than the direct team and is ratcheted up or down in size and scope based on the composition, stage, and duration of the incident.

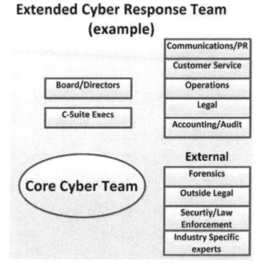

The extended team can be activated depending on the incident.

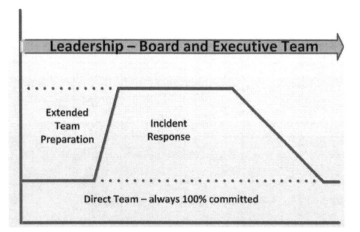

Managing the resources available for an attack is a key priority.

Specialized personnel resources: An important element in your preplanning for an incident response is to identify personnel in your organization with special skills that might be appropriate to a particular incident and insure that they have been incorporated into the planning process. For example, you might have a retired military officer who is very capable and well-trained in crisis response working in a separate, non-operational part of the organization. Knowing that skill exists in advance of an incident, and building these contingent resources into your response toolbox, may help you when an incident exceeds the scope of your normal response resources.

Actionable security intelligence versus audit/forensic data: Actionable data is information that is available in time to prevent or greatly reduce the impact of an intrusion. An example of this would be a tornado warning that gives you time to get into the basement or shelter. Audit data can be very important in the forensic reconstruction of an event, but does not help from a prevention standpoint. Having an audit trail showing precisely that 72 hours ago someone penetrated the system and made off with valuable information has some use in recovery and prosecution, but it is not helpful to the organization fighting to keep intruders out.

Real Time Situational Awareness (RTSA): Building a capability to monitor multiple areas of the organization in real time can be a valuable asset to your continual prevention efforts and allow cross-training and better utilization of resources worldwide. These solutions can link information from internal monitoring and control sources, open source news and alert feeds, social media, and proprietary information feeds. They can be presented through easy to use dashboards that can filter out the extraneous items and help analysts visualize issues through geographic, tabular, and other analytical data displays. An example of this is TIES (Trusted Information Exchange System) from Swan Island Networks – www.swanisland.net , a company I co-founded after the 9/11 attacks.

24/7: What is your attitude toward preparing and monitoring your information resources? Because of the global nature of cyber-attacks, your organization could be targeted any time of the day or night, weekday or weekends. Depending on the attack, different times might be more advantageous to the perpetrators – daytime high volume transaction activity could cover the movements of intruders if they are stealing small amounts of cash using ATM cards. In another instance, the middle of the night might be a more successful attack time because the expertise level of the monitoring personnel might be lower and more bandwidth available for large data downloads.

Command center(s):   Security Operation Centers (SOCs) have become much more common and formalized over the last 20 years, particularly in organizations that span the globe with their operations and facilities.   Many corporate command centers rival or exceed the capabilities of major government agencies.   When you compare Walmart with government centers, I would give the nod to Walmart in almost all instances – they are an impressive organization.   One element to examine inside your own organization is whether there are separate, parallel centers for cyber, network, and physical security operations – this can indicate a schism between departments that can be taken advantage of by a coordinated attack.   If a global organization has multiple command centers that can absorb primary incident responsibility during the prime time of their geographic area, this can help bolster redundancy, cross train key personnel, and better insure continuity of operations.   Microsoft demonstrated their SOC strategy at their 2011 Worldwide Public Safety Conference and it was very impressive in terms of proactive monitoring and the ability to instantly surge resources for a response.   The team was a combination of senior employees and dedicated contractors.

Layers of defense: It's likely that your team has defined a "defense in depth" strategy – multiple technologies designed to overlap and backstop security procedures in an attempt to keep intruders out or minimize the damage of an attack or intrusion. A working knowledge of these defensive elements is useful, and it's important to validate the created layers with outside, independent resources who may also utilize penetration-testing to actually stress the various parts of the system. It is important to realize that there can be gaps in even the deepest of defense systems, and one of your validation efforts should be to look for the gaps or areas where there may only be a thin layer of protection.

Training and certification: Continual training of your direct and extended team is an important element toward staying up to date and current on new threats that have emerged. It is also solid policy to continue to reinforce the existing capabilities and insure new members on your teams are fully capable of performing all required capabilities. Certification programs and cyber security degree programs are also becoming more available – it's important to insure that the knowledge gained is acted upon and kept current. One well-known training source is the SANS Institute (www.sans.org), which provides a wide range of instruction at many levels of the organization.

Exercises: Exercises that test the capabilities of the preparedness and prevention efforts of the teams will help insure a smooth response and validate existing process and policy. There are broad ranges of exercises that can be utilized, from repetitive and scheduled to unannounced and scenario-driven. Some exercises will involve groups and individuals well outside the immediate team, insuring that the capabilities tested can be deployed across the entire organization. Exercises should be done on a rotating schedule, with many smaller exercises leading up to a large-scale integrated exercise that stresses the entire organization.

Red teams: The concept of using a red team is to try to breach your own defenses with friendly intruders who work for your organization. Instead of stealing information or disrupting your organization's production, the red team takes note of the vulnerabilities they find and reports them to the internal team for evaluation and correction. It is far better to be embarrassed and exposed by your own efforts than to be on the front page of the *Wall Street Journal* explaining how you have been compromised by outside attackers. You can hire outside services that provide penetration testing and ongoing red teaming.

Monitoring: Detailed and continuous monitoring of your computing resources is a must. Many good products exist that will flag potential intrusions- this is hard, often times boring work for those tasked with maintaining a constant vigil – much like guard duty in the military. One continuing problem is the number of false alarms issued by the monitoring systems – the amount of information created can be massive and misleading. I had a monitoring tool that created such extensive audit logs that analyzing them took longer than was feasible for any actionable efforts. A key point on monitoring is stopping a problem in its tracks – while it is useful to understand when something happened by looking at the logs, it's far better to be proactive.

Real time response plan: You will need a real time response plan that will adapt to the changing nature of the threat. This plan will need to be available and followed by all those involved and incorporated into training and exercises. The plan will need to be updated on a regular basis and shared with trusted outside resources who will be mobilized in the event you need them for a major event. The plan should be a living, changing document that is continually updated and incorporates new threats or lessons learned. Dust on the binder is a sure sign that you have new threats that are not being accounted for.

Essential personnel: In every organization, there are essential personnel that you need to access 24/7. Many years ago, pagers were the alerting mechanism du jour, but this has migrated to mobile devices in most organizations. Multiple methods (calls, SMS, tweets, emails) to reach these people should be documented and tested and the information on the list rigorously maintained. The essential personnel list should be cross-organizational – the Chief Risk Officer might not be a network genius, but in a major attack will have specific issues that will need to be addressed.

"Kill Chain": I was told by a leading forensic and remediation firm that the average time an intruder is in a network before being discovered is 416 days. If true, this is a disheartening statistic and an important element to consider in your cyber defense thinking. Lockheed Martin has done a large amount of development work around this area of vulnerability, identifying the various stages that an attacker will go through when staging a breach attempt. If your defenses can disrupt the early stages of these attacks, you are in a far better position to minimize the damage or cause the intruder to go elsewhere. A physical example of this concept are motion detector lights around your house – if an intruder doing reconnaissance is suddenly bathed in light from every direction, he's likely to find a less well-defended property to burglarize.

Focus on the priorities: Your organization likely has a significant number of systems that do many different functions. In your preparedness plans, this is an important consideration – you want to allocate resources to the most important areas of the organization. A bank provides a good physical example – the vault is protected at a much higher level than the parking lot since all the major assets are put in the vault during off hours. Make sure your plans consider the different parts of your organization in priority order.

Alerting to all levels of the organization: Rapid and coordinated communications within the organization and with critical partners around the world is another important element of your preparation and prevention efforts. Alerts and notifications must be actionable and timely and directed to the correct community of recipients. Too much communication and the missives will be ignored; there are many systems that overload the recipients with reams of trivial information. However, not communicating broadly enough can also keep critical people out of the loop during a vital response period. If possible, an alerting system that can operate independently of the organization's formal system may be advantageous in the event of a major incident that demands shutting their primary systems down. There are multiple cloud-based providers of these services who can backstop your notification efforts at an effective price.

Multi-lingual/multi-cultural impact: If your organization is global, you may have incidents that have localized impact that affect different geographic customer groups differently. Your plans should include the ability to react in multiple languages and access to cultural norms that may be important to the response. Make this expertise part of your extended response team – either using internal resources or contracting in advance with an outside firm.

Documentation: An incident can be very fast-paced, confusing, and spread over a wide set of departments within the organization – in the physical world, this is known as the "fog of war." Within the incident response plan should be a planned method of capturing a full documentation stream of actions, activities, communications, and decisions – it will be important later as you wind down the incident and in the event you need to defend your actions with regulatory authorities and in the legal system.

Response budget and authority: The organization should budget for multiple types of responses necessary to attacks, and organize the authority to spend where necessary when an incident happens. If planned well, many of the needed resources will have been pre-contracted in advance, but there are always unique expenditures necessary that defy the planning process.

Planning fatigue: If your organization is doing a great job, your efforts at avoiding a major attack or breach may be successful – many times it is far easier for the potential intruders to shift their focus to another organization. If you have an extended period of calm, you may run into the situation where your key people start losing focus on the defenses and other things start to take up the time that was successfully utilized keeping you protected. It's important for executive management and the board to insure that there is a steady drumbeat of defensive activity and that reductions to those efforts are well thought out rather than done by default.

Post incident analysis planning: Your organization needs to plan how they will capture lessons learned and mistakes made during an incident. These procedures should be utilized as part of the organization's exercises and scenario planning as a means of insuring that they will be adequate in terms of capturing the information necessary to improve and resourced appropriately.

Re-planning triggers: As your organization changes, there will be events that happen that should cause you to reassess your preparedness plans and procedures, updating them as necessary. Some of these may include merger and acquisition activity, major new system deployments, new compliance or regulatory requirements, change in key leadership personnel, addition of new cybersecurity vendors, and the identification of major new threats. The key planner should be aware of these types of changes that are both internal and external to the organization's environment.

The SANS Institute's top cyber controls: The SANS Institute (www.sans.org) is an excellent resource for cyber security information. I've included a list of their 20 Critical Security Controls for your awareness and further research. Each is explained in a significant amount of detail on their site or with a free download of the full information around each item. Incorporating these controls into your preparedness and monitoring activities will help you cover the extensive ground that needs to be considered. Understanding the basics of each step to provide oversight to your technical team and organization is recommended.

SANS Institute 20 Critical Security Controls - Version 4.1 (www.sans.org)

- **Critical Control 1:** Inventory of Authorized and Unauthorized Devices

- **Critical Control 2:** Inventory of Authorized and Unauthorized Software

- **Critical Control 3:** Secure Configurations for Hardware and Software on Mobile Devices, Laptops, Workstations, and Servers

- **Critical Control 4:** Continuous Vulnerability Assessment and Remediation

- **Critical Control 5:** Malware Defenses

- **Critical Control 6:** Application Software Security

- **Critical Control 7:** Wireless Device Control

- **Critical Control 8:** Data Recovery Capability

- **Critical Control 9:** Security Skills Assessment and Appropriate Training to Fill Gaps

- **Critical Control 10:** Secure Configurations for Network Devices such as Firewalls, Routers, and Switches

- **Critical Control 11:** Limitation and Control of Network Ports, Protocols, and Services

- **Critical Control 12:** Controlled Use of Administrative Privileges

- **Critical Control 13:** Boundary Defense

- **Critical Control 14:** Maintenance, Monitoring, and Analysis of Audit Logs

- **Critical Control 15:** Controlled Access Based on the Need to Know

- **Critical Control 16:** Account Monitoring and Control

- **Critical Control 17:** Data Loss Prevention

- **Critical Control 18:** Incident Response and Management

- **Critical Control 19:** Secure Network Engineering

- **Critical Control 20:** Penetration Tests and Red Team Exercises

10 essential practices— cyber security defense in depth

Build a risk-aware culture

Manage incidents and respond

Defend the workplace

Security by design

Keep it clean

Control network access

Security in the clouds

Patrol the neighborhood

Protect the company jewels

Track who's who

Within each essential practice, move from manual and reactive to automated and proactive to achieve optimized security.

SOURCE: IBM Security Services Report

The IBM report cited is an excellent summary of a defense in-depth approach to information security inside an organization. Implementation is always challenging, especially in large and complex global organizations, but the alternative is far more painful to contemplate.

Plan Fundamentals

- Create & empower a team
- 24/7 "First Responders"
- Develop vendor and law enforcement relationships
- Create & document a plan
- Create a notification "tree"
- Create communication templates & scripts
- Develop on-call resources & remedies
- Employee training
- Regulatory & legal review
- Funding
- Ongoing critique

SOURCE: OTA 2013 Data Breach Readiness

Chapter 4 Key Points Summary:

Preparation and prevention are critical elements to a cyber-risk strategy – and may save you from a major incident.

Dedicated efforts should be allocated when possible to maximize the prevention element of your cyber threat efforts.

Early detection and elimination of an attacker can create a "kill chain" effect, keeping intruders from traversing from an initial entry point to other more sensitive system areas.

Outside resources are important to any preparation effort and comprehensive planning should be done to incorporate surge capabilities into the organization's plans.

Planning and exercising scenarios for incident response while things are calm will help when an actual event happens.

Outside validation of all preparedness and prevention steps is recommended – the organization should continue to cross check and second guess its efforts as a means to find gaps and add reinforcements.

Preparation is a never ending activity.

Preparation should span the entire organization – this is not an IT-only preparation effort.

Chapter 5: Attacked and Breached – Now What?

"Invincibility lies in the defence; the possibility of victory in the attack." - Sun Tzu

We've been breached or penetrated! These words will likely be communicated in most organizations soon, if they have not already been encountered in the past. Despite all the defenses and proactive measures available, the cyber area still presents a very broad attack surface, and your preparation and response will likely be tested under a real attack situation. Hopefully, you have done all the possible preparation work outlined in the previous chapter and can respond effectively. This chapter outlines broad guidance on how to handle an incident.

Anecdote - Checklists in Hospital Operating Rooms: Over the last several years, I've been monitoring a debate that has been recurring inside the healthcare community. The topic of the debate has been "checklist use" in complex procedures in the hospital operating room. I'm not a healthcare professional, but I would imagine that any complex procedure would be improved and risk reduced if multiple people had agreed on the key items ahead of time and verified those items on a checklist during the process. Many studies have come out that have cited strong improvement when checklists are utilized and some terrible results when they were not: wrong leg amputated, entirely different procedure performed, and other medical horror stories. I can't imagine that there ever would have been a debate over this course of action, but I have not worked extensively in this field. In my world, well thought-out and thoroughly tested checklists can be a lifesaver. Detailed checklists are recommended for your preparation and incident response.

A point in time: The very second that an incident is detected or reported, multiple streams of activity should unfold and continue to operate until it is determined that the crisis has been handled and mitigated – potentially years from the event occurring right now. Time is of the essence and seconds can count in terms of disrupting the damage taking place when an attack is first detected. Every incident will be different in its nature, but here are some general guidelines to think about as a base planning guide:

1. **Severity:** Cyber incidents can range from an irritation to a devastating loss. Understanding the range that a particular incident might cover is important to many aspects of the incident response. For example, a distributed denial of service or web site defacement both impact the organization, but don't expose data or other critical information to the outside world.

2. **Scope:** How widely does the attack or breach impact your organization and those that you have contact with? In the event you are in the business of storing and servicing other organization's records, this may be a critical determination for notification and disclosure activities that are time-sensitive.

3. **Type:** Breaches and attacks come in all shapes and sizes. If an employee calls in to say that he just had a laptop stolen out of his car and had downloaded 200,000 customer records for an analysis project, the impact and response will be vastly different from discovering an intruder with

privileged access to your network has been downloading highly-secured intellectual property.

4. **Affected data:** Understanding what type of data has been compromised is key – there are big differences between encrypted supply chain data and "in the clear" personally identifiable data (PII) about healthcare patients or retail customers. A rapid assessment followed up by detailed forensic analysis will be an important progression as the incident develops.

5. **Operational impact:** Do you know what impact the breach is going to have on your operations? Are you going to have to shut down mission critical systems for some period of time? Determining the potential impact will help coordinate activities and mobilize the right people in the organization.

6. **Legal impact**: It is important to correlate your industry regulations, compliance requirements, and other applicable legal requirements in order to understand how much legal effort is likely to be involved. It is important to give everyone the most lead time possible on response activities.

7. **Customer impact:** Are your customers already affected, or is the attack an internal breach only? If the attack was reported/identified by a customer, you will understand this immediately, but otherwise you will need to do an analysis to understand the possible impact on customers.

8. **Human resources impact**: If the incident involves internal employees or contractors, there are many personnel issues that will have to be addressed. Hopefully, one of your key responders will not be a malicious insider!

9. **Physical security impact**: If the incident involved a physical breach resulting in unauthorized access to sensitive facilities such as data centers or laboratories, it will be important to involve your security personnel to fix

the access problem, insure no continuing access is happening, and gathering evidence from access control systems, video surveillance systems, and security logs. Not all attacks will come through the same channel.

10. **Partner impact:** You may have partners that are affected – interlocking of systems is becoming far more common in the race to speed throughput and maximize information sharing.

11. **Law Enforcement:** Understanding when you need to involve law enforcement is another critical element of assessing the breach. Different attacks will demand different involvement from law enforcement.

12. **Sharing:** You may not be the only organization under the attack scenario that your organization is experiencing. If you share information around the event, you may find others that you can collaborate with on remediation, or save another organization from a similarly structured attack.

Immediate plan execution: Like many pro football teams' game starting strategy, your first 15-25 process steps to initiate when a compromise is detected should be scripted on a checklist that has been very well thought-out, tested and validated both internally and by outside experts. Confusion will likely be a significant factor in many cases; there will be usually be key people out of the loop, many of them if the incident is happening at midnight on a weekend night. It is also imperative that the person in charge has immediate access to the attack response plan. If this basic process isn't well-honed, something is already going very wrong in your response to an attack or breach.

The items below are a basic set of activities that can be a starting point for your organizational planning process. Your organization should have spent a significant amount of time developing, verifying and exercising this checklist specific to your organization's situation.

Immediate initial assessment (First 4 hours):

1. **Stop the damage being done and prevent further damage if possible:** This is often called a containment strategy. If you have done your preparation well, your organization will have a clear understanding of how various systems are connected and have anticipated how to contain a breach from multiple vectors.

2. **Verify the incident as thoroughly as possible:** Ensure that the breach or attack is well understood and that you understand the impact and scope thoroughly. There could be multiple attacks going on at the same time, with one being a distraction and a more serious attack happening under the radar of the monitoring/analysis.

3. **Understand and communicate the scope and nature of the incident internally:** Getting the right people in the communications loop is a key factor to deploying your strategy. One important element is a means for people joining into the incident to get briefed without having the incident manager re-explain the situation verbally to many different people. This can completely consume the person trying to make decisions about what to do and slow the response process.

4. **Notify extended team participants:** As you understand the scope and urgency of the incident, you will need to decide who to notify and activate for the response. If you have done your preparation well, your organization will have access to all your pre-contracted vendors, and the individuals who will have the responsibility for notifying

those vendors. You may also have internal extended team members to activate depending on the circumstances.

5. **Isolate the systems involved where applicable:** Isolating the attacked or breached systems can be a very complex process depending on operational constraints, regulations and a litany of other factors. Your organization should have a very good set of documentation on how to accomplish this already prepared to ease the panicked decision-making process that can occur without proper preparation.

6. **Start a forensics collection process:** Preserve all the evidence possible. Understanding how to collect evidence of the breach is another vital area of your response. The information will be immediately important to mitigation and recovery. You may also need detailed forensics for insurance, law enforcement, disclosure decisions and after action reviews.

7. **Begin a detailed, comprehensive documentation process**: Memories will fade quickly, so you will want a good record of events for your after action analysis and reports, This record will help with any law enforcement or litigation process that comes up. In your preparation, this role should be assigned to someone outside the critical decision making loop to minimize the impact on the incident responders.

As the incident evolves, there will be many variables that emerge out of the details of the attack that will have to be factored into the overall response plan. Reconfiguring the team to fit the new circumstances will be an important part of your effort. Preplanning and realistic exercises will create agility and resilience for your organization when a real attack happens.

As the incident develops: Once your response begins, things can get complex very quickly. There may be many elements that are changing rapidly that you should evaluate and monitor, and multiple parts of the organization will be involved. Below are some general guidelines on items that may affect you, and have an impact on the quality of your response:

1. **Communicate effectively!** Your team will need to move information between internal groups and a dynamic set of outside entities. This information will range from the strategic (e.g. SEC disclosure discussions) to the mundane (e.g. website copy revisions). I recommend that these channels be set up and practiced during exercises, and that there is a good effort to avoid duplication and conflicting information. You will need to ensure that there are multiple communications channels operating simultaneously, and that appropriate information is shared with the right groups and individuals. This will help to minimize the amount of information and help you consider who should have access to what material.

2. **Improve and enhance the initial assessment:** Your initial assessment of the attack will likely improve greatly as information is analyzed and communicated. Summarizing changes as they are understood and distributing a succinct update will help focus everyone involved. Many organizations find that time-stamping or a numeric identifier helps insure that the latest information is utilized.

3. **Establish an incident manager/commander with authority to handle full incident response:** If the breach is significant and involves many different groups across the organization, you will need to organize the command and control elements based on the composition of the incident at hand. If you've prepared well in advance, this will happen almost automatically, but for organizations not well

prepared, this activity can result in confusion, politics, and competing interests all at the wrong time.

4. **Confirm critical organizational team members' availability and connection status**: Your organization will have a plan, but it is likely that something will go wrong. There may be a critical team member who just left for four weeks on a sabbatical and is unreachable, or another key person might be unavailable for other reasons. I had an incident in the 90's where I was on a runway 3,000 miles away, so was out of the loop for at least six hours. My key response manager did an incredible job managing the incident until he accidently cut the tip of his finger off and had to go to the hospital. Having a plan with multiple layers of back-up personnel can be very helpful if things take an unexpected turn.

5. **Mobilize contracted outside resources as appropriate:** You should have a set of resources that are pre-contracted before an event – either through a retainer with a guaranteed level of service or a pre-negotiated services contract. You will need to decide which entities are necessary and coordinate their level of response. These resources can be the critical "surge" that you'll need during the most active part of the incident; adding both expertise and depth to your internal team.

6. **Investigation:** You'll need a strategy for investigating the attack circumstances. This may be done internally, with law enforcement, using outside service providers, or a combination of all of these. Your internal legal organization will likely be heavily involved along with a number of other departments that will need to document and communicate the results.

7. **Determine ongoing impact of the response:** Your organization is unlikely to stop everything else while the incident is resolved, so it will be important to estimate the

impact upon the overall organization, while reserving the right to increase the requirements as needed:

a. **Board and Management:** If you've had a significant incident, it may demand a high level of attention by your C-suite executives and members of the board of directors. Recent attacks have seen the CEO having to be the face of the organization to the media and customers for a significant amount of time. Highly visible attacks or a breach that impacts the long-term future of the company (e.g. intellectual property theft) can demand multiple board meetings to properly frame and respond.

b. **IT/Technical:** An attack can shutter critical systems or be the trigger for an unplanned, major overhaul of technology to recover and remediate the issues uncovered by the breach. This type of requirement could send shockwaves throughout the organization and take many months or years to fully resolve. This type of event would undoubtedly impact other priorities inside the organization.

c. **Operations:** The operating elements of the company can be similarly affected depending on the scope and size of the attack. Established ways of operating might need major changes, causing retraining of personnel and reconfiguring of processes across wide areas of the organization.

d. **Legal:** Your legal department may have to live with the outcome of a breach for multiple years. Beyond the initial response, there may be areas where prosecution of the attackers will demand substantial participation by the organization, taking years to work its way through the legal system and crossing multiple jurisdictional boundaries. On the opposite end, the organization may receive legal action against it for the breach: shareholder lawsuits, class action lawsuits and a host of other actions by individuals and groups harmed (or positioning themselves as harmed) by the incident. There may also be complex insurance claims that will require action by the legal resources of the company.

e. **Customers:** Your customers are critical to your long-term success as an organization, and there may be heavy impact on the relationship depending on the severity of the incident. Notification, rebuilding of trust, ongoing communications and an array of ongoing actions like credit protection may be required to remediate the impact of the attack.

f. **Media:** Cyber-attacks are terrific news events for the media covering the organization, generating many stories and in-depth follow-up investigations. You will need to assess and plan for the impact across your organization.

g. **Law Enforcement:** Law enforcement has been responding to the increased number of cyber-attacks by increasing its expertise and the size of the organizations responding to attacks. An attack will result in the need to support investigations and hopefully prosecution of the perpetrators.

h. **Partners/Vendors**: Your organization partners can be impacted greatly and you may need to allocate significant organizational resources to assist in this process.

i. **Regulators:** Your organization is subject to regulations, likely from many different sources. It may take significant effort to understand all of the areas where you will need to respond; I'd recommend a proactive strategy of identifying all the entities you will need to interact with.

Post-incident analysis: A critical part of any attack or breach is a review of the incident and an analysis of the response efforts. This should be undertaken when the incident has been handled and is not demanding massive time commitments across the organization, but soon enough after to ensure that everyone's memory of the incident is still sharp.

The makeup of the review will depend on multiple factors. You may want to keep the review internal to the organization or invite involved outside resources to participate. You can also decide to hold multiple reviews focusing on different levels of the organizational activities. All of the information should be accumulated and reviewed by management or the board depending on the severity and impact.

Part of the incident response effort should have been extensive documentation that can be summarized for the post event review. These reviews can be very uncomfortable and confrontational, but efforts should be made to get constructive feedback rather than a finger-pointing set of blame accusations. I would recommend a very senior executive or board member moderates the session and encourages feedback from all directions. This is a very valuable learning opportunity and should cover a variety of issues. I have posed some sample questions that might be useful in the review:

Attack/breach cause and impact:

- Did we identify the attacker?
- Did we identify the method of attack?
- What was the short term and long term impact?

- Is there a clear responsibility/blame point inside the organization for the attack?
- Was the attack preventable if we had taken different defense actions?
- Did other organizations outside of ours suffer the same attack?
- Was there an internal violation of our defenses or policy?
- Was an inside employee involved? A trusted outsider?
- Can we determine how long the intruders were in our system?
- Were account credentials stolen?
- Could there be any residual elements remaining?
- Did the attack spread outside our organization network – to partners or customers?

Incident response review:

- Did our initial response plan work well?
- Did our plan anticipate this type of attack?
- Did we communicate well throughout the incident?
- Did our outside vendors and services respond as contracted?
- Who did we have to involve in the response that was unanticipated?
- Were there any severe disagreements over responsibility or control?
- Were we able to preserve operational security without leaks to undesired sources?
- Did we get the right levels of management involved at the right time?
- What was the public, customer, or partner perspective of the attack?

- Did we do the right level of information sharing with appropriate outsiders?
- Did we comply with all the proper regulatory issues?

Lessons learned:

- What did we do that was excellent and well-executed?
- What employees or outside resources distinguished themselves during the incident?
- What was completely unanticipated or went extremely poorly?
- What deployment of personnel would you do differently next time?
- How have other organizations handled similar incidents and what can we incorporate?

Corrective actions already taken: Creating a list of direct and indirect actions already taken as the incident transpired will give everyone in the review a good sense of progress made. Sometimes the good that comes out of an incident due to the focus of an attack can outweigh the consequences.

Corrective recommendations for future: This is an important part of the review process and should go through a detailed thought process. The recommendations will likely affect budgets, personnel and priorities in the coming months and years. It is important to tie all these actions into the overall preparedness planning and insure that the recommendations are realistic for the organization – just like New Year's resolutions, making the list of desired changes is significantly easier than actually executing the changes.

Impact on the preparedness plan: The post-incident review will identify areas in your plan that requires improvement and reconsideration in order to optimize your response to future incidents.

The post-incident review can pay large dividends and help your entire organization improve its defenses and response capabilities. It is always unfortunate to have to examine where things went wrong, but a positive attitude toward improving everything possible in the event that another attack occurs can be a lifesaver.

Sharing your lessons learned with organizations you trust can also pay dividends as the exchange can generate a mutual give and take on best practices and prevention techniques, as well as ways to improve your incident response capabilities.

Chronology of a breach – Target, 2013

I woke up on December 19, 2013 to the news that Target had a massive breach and data theft. The news coverage was extensive; outside "sources" were detailing that 40 million credit cards had been compromised, likely over the Black Friday shopping period (the day after Thanksgiving) and that Target was not responding to media inquiries. The initial report had come from an outside security blogger (http://krebsonsecurity.com), who reported that Target was investigating a potential breach on December 13, six days before the major story broke and the statement from Target that was issued shortly thereafter.

Target confirmed the investigation through a public statement early in the morning of the 19th, giving details that the data was stolen during a period of a couple of weeks starting with Thanksgiving and was isolated to point-of-sale users in U.S. stores – online shoppers were not affected. The Chairman and CEO was quoted in the statement, "Target's first priority is preserving the trust of our guests and we have moved swiftly to address this issue, so guests can shop with confidence. We regret any inconvenience this may cause," said Gregg Steinhafel, chairman, president and chief executive officer, Target. "We take this matter very seriously and are working with law enforcement to bring those responsible to justice."

I had been to Target and used my credit card during the period of the breach and have been monitoring my statements for any sign of misuse or fraud. Fortunately, no use has occurred, though I'll continue to monitor.

The Target website was updated with detailed information about credit reports, exploited customer information, and state specific implications. A number to call was provided for concerned customers. The company asserted that a leading forensics team would be called in to assist and that they were working with law enforcement and taking additional steps to prevent this in the future.

Target's public stock price was not heavily affected in first day of trading following the announcement of the breach, decreasing only 2% in market trading on the day of the announcement. Ten days later, the stock was still stable, despite media reports that the insurance cost of all 40 million credit cards could cost Target $1.5 billion dollars. On January 29th, the stock had lost over 10% of its value, gradually declining from the point of the attack announcement. While the percentage doesn't sound too bad in light of the major news, that decrease represents approximately $4 billion in reduction to the company's total market capitalization.

Further stories about the attack detailed that the criminals had compromised point-of-sale terminals in the United States and Canada to capture the information – implying that the main data systems were not breached. Banks like J.P. Morgan announced their support of Target, opening their call centers to cardholders who were worried. This help from partners is an important element of the financial system – which is a very delicate, complicated infrastructure that the entire world depends upon. J.P. Morgan limited the cash withdrawal and credit limits of affected debit and credit cards, angering many of its customers who were still doing their Christmas shopping.

The initial notification and response by Target's senior executives and P.R. department seemed very well thought-out and comprehensive in nature. The CEO of the company, in a red logoed Target polo shirt, was heartfelt in his apologies and gave customers an additional 10% discount for two days in the stores. He also assured the customers that they would not suffer any financial harm and that Target was working hard to improve the situation and eliminate the possibility of this happening again.

In subsequent weeks, there was some media controversy over the PIN (Personal Identification Numbers) for debit cards that was not handled well in my opinion. The company was steadfast that the PINS had not been compromised because they had been triple-encrypted and stored separately from the other information. The media continued to paint the scenario of a team of hackers working on the encrypted files to obtain the PINS. Explaining to the public the fine distinctions was very difficult. Yes, the information was stolen, but no, it hadn't been compromised because it was triple-encrypted is a detailed and technical point to get across when your trust, as well as your systems, have been decimated by intruders.

From a security and incident response standpoint, the fact that an outside security blogger was privy to the investigation would be worrisome to me in terms of operational security. You don't want to have others releasing information ahead of your planned statements if you can help it. One of my post incident action items would be examining how that information was obtained, whether through an employee or an outside vendor and whether the proper policies were in place to govern the controls of this type of information.

There was much speculation after the incident in terms of the attack and whether Target was in compliance with the credit card security standard PCI DSS, which has detailed standards for storing and keeping specific information. A red flag was the fact that the codes from the back of the card were stolen, the storing of which is reportedly against the standards of the PCI framework. There was also much theorizing that the incident had to be partly enabled by an insider to Target – not a pleasant prospect to try to validate and locate the individual. The breach will cost Target millions, but it seems that because these events are happening with fairly regular frequency, few people will switch their habits, particularly when the financial systems absorbs all of the fraudulent transactions.

More bad news: In mid-January, Target released a stunning update to their public disclosure about the data breach. In addition to the 40 million credit cards that had been compromised through their point-of-sale system, Target announced that up to 70 million other customers had their information compromised: emails, addresses, phone numbers and more. This newly announced breach went beyond the point-of-sale system and impacted other classes of customers. Surprisingly to me, Target's public stock has been largely unaffected.

From a company press release: "At this time, the Company is not able to estimate the costs, or a range of costs, related to the data breach. Costs may include liabilities to payment card networks for reimbursements of credit card fraud and card reissuance costs, liabilities related to Target's proprietary REDCard fraud and card re-issuance, liabilities from civil litigation, governmental investigations and enforcement proceedings, expenses for legal, investigative and consulting fees, and incremental expenses and capital investments for remediation activities. These costs may have a material adverse effect on Target's results of operations in fourth quarter 2013 and/or future periods."

I would encourage you to follow the long term outcome of this breach to understand if there are parallels within your organization that you can learn from, incorporating the best ideas into your preparedness planning and utilizing some of the areas that parallel your organization's scenarios within your preparatory exercises to add realism and complexity. There have already been a significant number of lawsuits filed, which will cost the company a significant amount of money in legal defense fees even if they are judged harmless in these actions.

Chapter 5 Key Points Summary:

Incidents are going to happen – be thoroughly prepared in advance.

Time is of the essence in a response. Everyone should have a great sense of urgency without panicked behavior. You can develop this through exercises and pre-planning.

There should be a very clear, practiced response plan for the initial moments of any attack that is available to the personnel most likely to be involved at the moment the attack is detected.

Practice through drills and exercises with the team that will handle actual incidents, shifting roles and responsibilities to account for changing personnel schedules. You are not going to know in advance when incidents will occur.

Plan and exercise your surge response where outside vendors and flexible internal resources are mobilized.

Contract the surge resources that you need outside ahead of time so they can respond without delay. Build service level agreements with clear response times outlined.

Insure your communications are streamlined and organized so that the incident manager does not have to re-explain the basic situation many different times.

Make every attempt to preserve the evidence of the attack - it will be important for immediate and long-term elements of the incident recovery.

Document all of your actions – memories will fade quickly. The lawyers and regulators won't fade away.

Take the time and make a concerted effort to perform a post-incident review where everyone summarizes their learning and improves the future defensive effort.

Get as many people across the organization involved in assessing impact - there are likely many variables that need to be considered. This is much more than an IT problem.

Chapter 6: Cyber Information Sharing

"Talent is always conscious of its own abundance, and does not object to sharing." - Aleksandr Solzhenitsyn

Anecdote - The Yellowstone Ecosystem: In 1995, the grey wolf was reintroduced into Yellowstone National Park amidst a lot of hope by the endangered species constituency, along with an equal amount of consternation by the ranchers and farmers who feared new risks of their cattle being attacked. The wolf population has thrived and the overall project is considered by most to be a success. Inherent in the wolves behavior in the park is a valuable lesson that relates to our discussion of cyber information sharing. The wolves have two major sources of protein available to their packs: buffalo and elk. Both the elk and buffalo have thrived inside Yellowstone over the years with the absence of natural predators. The wolves eat significantly more elk than buffalo because of the different response to a wolf attack. The elk, when attacked, scatter in virtually an "every elk for himself " panic. If one of the elk has a gimpy leg, they can be isolated from the others by the wolves and eaten for breakfast – good the Darwin principal, bad for that one elk. The buffalo, in most cases, have a different response to the wolves – when the buffalo sense danger, they communicate that sense, circle the herd, and align the most capable defenses facing outward. ___All the buffalo are afforded an enhanced level of protection through a shared communication about danger.___

If that story doesn't give you an immediate desire to start sharing cyber security information to equalize the malicious threats across the many partner organizations you are linked to, return this book for credit and go on alone ☺. Just hope and pray you are not the one with the compromised limb when the herd scatters and the predators show up!

If you see the common sense aspect of sharing threat information, that is a good start toward the actions required to make sharing happen. Information sharing is complicated, political, hard to sustain, and fraught with policy issues. Despite the effort needed, it is one of the best things that legitimate organizations can do to leverage their efforts to combat the growing cyber arsenal of threats. The synergistic efforts of everyone on the good side of the equation will put pressure on those looking to exploit our current situation. There is truly strength in numbers.

One of the most indelible examples of information sharing failure was 9/11 and the attacks on the World Trade Center in New York, the Pentagon in Washington, D.C. and the Pennsylvania countryside where Flight 93 crashed. The 9/11 Commission underscored the failure to "connect the dots" in multiple ways, and entirely new segments of government emerged in response. The creation of the state and local "intelligence fusion" centers were accomplished and have been proceeding in fits and starts for 10 years. The government is still trying to improve the level and speed of sharing in the physical security realm, and there is much work to do. Cyber sharing is even less advanced in late 2013, but is advancing rapidly on a number of initiatives.

Sharing imperative: We are all stronger and more resilient if we work together. It is imperative to start the effort toward sharing, starting with easy, high level sharing, and adding layers and capabilities until you get to real time sharing of technical indicators at machine speeds. There are many organizations you can share with and I would implore you to look at how you can enable this critical communication channel in an expeditious manner. We've discussed in depth defense strategies in terms of systems and intrusion detection, consider a "sharing in depth" strategy with overlapping levels of sharing and a broad set of disparate sharing partners. This will allow you to build a very strong situational awareness picture that will be continually enhanced with real world information.

Sharing objections: As you discuss sharing information within your organization, you will encounter a set of objections that should all be considered, but overcome in a way that allows sharing without further damaging the organization or exposing proprietary information. The lawyers will worry about litigation and sensitive information transfer. The risk officer might be concerned about disclosure issues that may result if you share too broadly. The CEO might worry about bad publicity or brand damage if something shared leaks out. The board can examine all these issues and help arbitrate a good middle ground that will assuage the doubters and empower the collaborators. The slide below from PwC, one of the leading worldwide consulting and audit firms, shows a summary of reasons against sharing cited in their information security research:

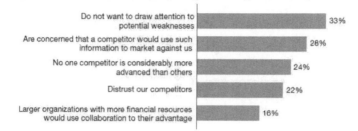

Figure 12: Reasons for not collaborating on information security

SOURCE: PWC Defending Yesterday, Key Findings from the Global State of Information Security® Survey 2014

The board of directors is positioned in a unique way to assist in sharing efforts. Most board members hold multiple board seats across different companies, creating a natural network of high level business professionals with strong trust relationships. Information and best practices shared between companies will lighten the load for all and enable many different views and communication channels. You should not violate any protected confidences, but rather determine where you can share and work those angles that are mutually beneficial. Board members should ensure that they understand the limitations of sharing. For written documents, they could utilize the Traffic Light Protocol (TLP), defined below, as a way of limiting distribution beyond their comfort zone.

There are many aspects of information sharing and the impediments can be formidable, especially in an environment where it's more comfortable and convenient to stay insulated. Let's look at some of the different ways your organization can benefit and participate in information sharing efforts:

High level communication: There are a significant number of conferences and organizations that have working groups, conferences, and do significant research for the benefit of the industry. When these opportunities present themselves, I would encourage you to participate, understanding the rules under which the information you contribute will be used. If a conference is being broadcast and digitally recorded, the statements made by representatives of your organization could be on YouTube for decades to come. If you look at the survey results published by groups like Deloitte and Ponemon, they poll thousands of organizations on detailed issues but publish the results in an aggregated form that does not compromise individual company's information. This high level sharing provides an immense amount of information to others fighting the same battles.

Security note: There are many firms that aggregate and publish incident and breach information in highly useful summaries. I have not heard of a research firm's data being compromised by a cyber-attack, but having detailed survey results for thousands of global companies in a database would be an attractive target if I was a cyber-criminal. You might want to check the survey agreement for specifics on how this information is maintained and protected. This kind of detailed understanding is important to monitor with any information that is held in someone else's environment.

Industry sharing: If your organization is part of a defined industry group like financial services, energy, transportation, retail or others, you likely have access to sharing mechanisms that have been organized to aid collaboration inside a specific group. This can be very important when there is specific compliance or regulatory elements that are unique to a particular industry segment. An example is the PCI DSS (Payment Card Industry Data Security Standard – a highly developed set of conventions and standards that bolster the security of the entire payment card ecosystem.) The ISACs (Information Sharing and Analysis Centers) provide a framework for industries to collaborate – with varying results by industry. The National Council of ISACS www.isaccouncil.org has links to all the industry specific groups that are organized under their charter. Department of Homeland Security has identified 16 areas of critical infrastructure and maintains information relevant to each.

From the ISAC website: "The National Council of ISACs, formerly known as the ISAC Council, was formed in 2003 when a volunteer group of ISAC representatives decided to meet monthly to develop trusted relationships among the sectors and to address common issues and concerns. The National Council of ISACs activities include: drills and exercises, hosting a private sector liaison at the Department of Homeland Security (DHS) National Infrastructure Coordinating Center (NICC) during incidents of national significance, emergency classified briefings, and real-time sector threat level reporting. The group also sponsors an annual Critical Infrastructure Protection (CIP) Congress to bring together the critical infrastructure community for networking, learning and addressing issues of concern to CIKR stakeholders.

- Chemical
- Commercial Facilities
- Communications
- Critical Manufacturing
- Dams
- Defense Industrial Base
- Emergency Services
- Energy
- Financial Services
- Food and Agriculture
- Government Facilities
- Healthcare and Public Health
- Information Technology
- Nuclear Reactors, Materials, and Waste
- Transportation Systems
- Water and Wastewater Systems

SOURCE: Department of Homeland Security

Traffic Light Protocol (TLP): US CERT (United States Computer Emergency Readiness Team), part of the Department of Homeland Security, has adopted TLP, which originated in the United Kingdom's National Infrastructure Security Co-ordination Centre (**NISCC**) as a means of coordinating sharing across many organizations. It is a set of recommended conventions around sharing sensitive information, also employed by public- and private-sector organizations within Australia, Canada, Finland, France, Germany, Hungary, Italy, Japan, Netherlands, New Zealand, Norway, Sweden, and Switzerland.

It is important to understand that this is a trust-based method of sharing – there are no technology constraints or automated processes that prevent someone from disregarding the sharing levels described below. Nonetheless, it is a very well thought-out structure that can be adopted by many sharing organizations in lieu of creating yet another unique method or doing nothing to control the dissemination of information.

Color	When should it be used?	How may it be shared?
RED	Sources may use TLP: RED when information cannot be effectively acted upon by additional parties, and could lead to impacts on a party's privacy, reputation, or operations if misused.	Recipients may not share TLP: RED information with any parties outside of the specific exchange, meeting, or conversation in which it is originally disclosed.
AMBER	Sources may use TLP: AMBER when information requires support to be effectively acted upon, but carries risks to privacy, reputation, or operations if shared outside of the organizations involved.	Recipients may only share TLP: AMBER information with members of their own organization who need to know, and only as widely as necessary to act on that information.
GREEN	Sources may use TLP: GREEN when information is useful for the awareness of all participating organizations as well as with peers within the broader community or sector.	Recipients may share TLP: GREEN information with peers and partner organizations within their sector or community, but not via publicly accessible channels.
WHITE	Sources may use TLP: WHITE when information carries minimal or no foreseeable risk of misuse, in accordance with applicable rules and procedures for public release.	TLP: WHITE information may be distributed without restriction, subject to copyright controls.

SOURCE: Department of Homeland Security

Transactional structured information sharing: Much of the exciting innovations underway in the sharing of cyber threat information are happening in the area of automated exchange of data transactions using structured information techniques and standardized formats. XML (Extensible Markup Language) was made part of the internet in the late 90's, and has spawned an entire industry around creating and implementing automated structured communications that can be used by the world to streamline information flow. The widespread adoption of these vocabularies will have a significant impact in the coming years. Below are a couple of well-developed examples that are a harbinger of things to come in the cyber world:

XBRL (Extensible Business Reporting Language): XBRL is built around the idea that accounting and business report information should not have to be re-entered and should be consumable by computer systems as well as individuals. Charlie Hoffman innovated the initial idea in 1998, and since then, XBRL has been adopted worldwide as a means of accelerating information flow across every organization dealing with business reporting. If you have read some of the mind-numbing detail in an annual report looking for one or two facts, you'll understand the power this type of structured information sharing can enable.

Common Alerting Protocol (CAP): CAP was the brainchild of Art Botterell in California, who was equally frustrated that there was no uniform method that could be utilized across the multitude of information sources available to him in the California emergency response arena. OASIS, a leading standards body, created an emergency management committee, and has taken CAP, with the help of the Emergency Interoperability Consortium, to worldwide adoption in a little over 10 years. In the United States, NOAA, FEMA, FCC all utilize CAP in some way to provide real time alerting. Internationally, Europe, Australia, Canada, and organizations like the World Meteorological Organization have implemented CAP programs. Even developing nations like Sri Lanka are implementing this very useful capability. OASIS (www.oasis-open.com) is the global standards group that facilitated CAP's development and has additional emergency management standards available and under development.

In the cyber threat world, there are numerous initiatives under way to structure and automate the sharing and dissemination of different types of alert and incident information in real time. I will highlight the main efforts, which are originating from government, consortiums and the private sector. This is an area to monitor closely, and I would recommend a "lean forward" approach toward experimentation and incorporation.

I have avoided a deep technical dive into these emerging standards, opting to point you to areas on the web where you can obtain detailed information if you are inclined to pursue these in depth. The standards groups all harness great support from external organizations and the public, and take a long term view toward making these standards both operable and interoperable. They also solicit comments from the public. This can make progress slow, but a good standard can unify a wide variety of efforts and streamline a difficult process.

OpenIOC: OpenIOC is an XML schema created by Mandiant, one of the leading companies in the cyber response market, and recently acquired by FireEye, one of the premier cyber security device manufacturers. Mandiant is based in the Washington D.C. area and has been instrumental in identifying the underlying cause and perpetrators of many successful attacks. Mandiant has taken this capability developed for internal use and made it available as a sharing method that can be used globally. The goals, in common with initiatives like STIX, are to speed the analysis and decision-making process by automating various elements of the process. IOC stands for Indicators of Compromise and there are over 500 distinct indicators that are available within the OpenIOC framework. I like this standard because it is being utilized every day by a company that is continually working the issues and encountering new attack indicators that can be tracked and shared.

From an OpenIOC whitepaper:

"OpenIOC is a format for recording, defining, and sharing information that allows your organization to accomplish this by sharing many different types of threat information both internally and externally in a machine-digestible format. OpenIOC is an open and flexible standard that can be modified on the fly as additional intelligence is gathered so that you can capture input from human subject matter experts and translate it into a format that can be used by various technologies to sweep your enterprise for signs that it has been compromised or is currently under attack to combat advanced targeted attacks in a manner that makes real remediation a realizable goal and enhances your security posture to combat future intrusions."

STIX (Structured Threat Information eXpression): STIX is under development by MITRE, a non-profit, federally funded organization with a long history of innovative research and smart people working in the public interest. MITRE welcomes collaboration and input on the evolving nature of the structures which will ultimately allow sharing across the entire range of cyber information and use cases. There is an exhaustive amount of information on the MITRE site dedicated to STIX. The information below is directly from an overview paper on STIX's capabilities:

STIX provides a common mechanism for addressing structured cyber threat information across and among this full range of use cases improving consistency, efficiency, interoperability, and overall situational awareness. In addition, STIX provides a unifying architecture tying together a diverse set of cyber threat information including:

- Cyber Observables
- Indicators
- Incidents
- Adversary Tactics, Techniques, and Procedures
- Exploit Targets (e.g., vulnerabilities, weaknesses or configurations)
- Courses of Action
- Cyber Attack Campaigns
- Cyber Threat Actors

TAXII (Trusted Automated eXchange of Indicator Information): TAXII is also under development by MITRE as the main transport mechanism for STIX information. Once the TAXII services are full developed, organizations will have the technical ability to share complex cyber threat information in an automated and secure manner. There will need to be a "trust network" or multiple sharing networks developed by participants to augment the technical capabilities – as noted earlier, policy and agreement on how to share are important elements in any exchange relationship.

IODEF (Incident Object Description Exchange Format): IODEF is an IETF MILE working group initiative aimed at defining an information framework to represent incidents from computer and network security systems. RFC5070 is the IETF designator for this effort, and extensive information is available on the web.

MILE (Managed Incident Lightweight Exchange): is an IETF (Internet Engineering Task Force) working group that is developing IODEF and RID as a global mechanism for categorizing and sharing incident information. MILE is an exchange standard that facilitates the trusted transfer of information between parties.

RID (Real time Internetwork Defense): RID is another IETF protocol that facilitates information exchange in the cyber arena. Information can be found under the IETF designator RFC 6545.

VERIS (Vocabulary for Event Recording and Incident Sharing): Verizon has developed a very good standard format for sharing incident reports and the download address is listed in the resource section. Their 2013 Data Breach Investigations Report is a wealth of knowledge. They have opened their methodology to the world to use and I would encourage an evaluation of the VERIS framework within your organization. VERIS draws upon a wealth of partners for its research and report, including (sourced directly from report):

• Australian Federal Police (AFP)
• CERT Insider Threat Center at the CMU Software Engineering Institute (CERT) (U.S.)
• Consortium for Cybersecurity Action (U.S.)
• Danish Ministry of Defence, Center for Cybersecurity
• Danish National Police, NITES (National IT Investigation Section)
• Deloitte (U.S.)
• Dutch Police: National High Tech Crime Unit (NHTCU)
• Electricity Sector Information Sharing and Analysis Center (ES-ISAC) (U.S.)
• European Cyber Crime Center (EC3)
• G-C Partners, LLC (U.S.)
• Guardia Civil (Cybercrime Central Unit) (Spain)

- Industrial Control Systems Cyber Emergency Response Team (ICS-CERT)
- Irish Reporting and Information Security Service (IRISS-CERT)
- Malaysia Computer Emergency Response Team (MyCERT), CyberSecurity Malaysia
- National Cybersecurity and Communications Integration Center (NCCIC) (U.S.)
- ThreatSim (U.S.)
- U.S.Computer Emergency Readiness Team (US-CERT)
- U.S.Secret Service (USSS)

From a Verizon whitepaper: VERIS is designed to provide a common language for describing security incidents in a structured and repeatable manner. It takes the narrative of "who did what to what (or whom) with what result" and translates it into the kind of data you see in this report. Because we hope to facilitate the tracking and sharing of security incidents, we released VERIS for free public use.

Government sharing efforts: I will cover the various agencies inside the U.S. Federal Government that disseminate information in a later chapter. The government witnessed firsthand on 9/11 that failure to "connect the dots" of existing and known information can have devastating consequences. The government is trying to share on a number of different agency fronts, but I would consider them one channel only, and continue to develop other methods for sharing within your organizational strategy. The government is also trying to enable information standards that will help unify the sharing efforts across the public and private sector. MITRE has been tasked to develop TAXII as one standard, and NIST has been tasked with creating a voluntary cyber framework as part of the executive order issued by the White House. All are well-intentioned efforts, but will likely fall short in terms of delivery, real time speed, and usefulness unless they can convince the private sector to actively adopt, utilize and help improve subsequent versions.

Global Risk Network (GRN): The Global Risk Network is a non-profit consortium based out of New York University (www.nyu.edu/intercep/grn/). The Global Risk Network is a consortium of leading international corporations and their senior executives that have formed a trusted network to address emerging disruptive forces - representing both threats and opportunities - that may impact their global activities. The organization provides a number of ways for member organizations to communicate through face-to-face meetings and electronic outreach. Membership is by invitation, likely to keep the trust level high.

Chapter 6 Key Points Summary:

Information sharing is a high payoff, underutilized defense mechanism against cyber attackers.

Sharing can be done at many levels and at many different degrees of information disclosure.

Trust is a key element to a sharing program. Establish strong ties and honor the rules set by your trusted partners.

Investigate your industry ISAC (Information Sharing and Analysis Center) – some are excellent sources of sharing and collaboration and can assist you significantly.

You may need people with security clearances to get very sensitive information from the U.S. Federal Government. This is likely worth the effort for large organizations.

Understand the legal and regulatory issues in sharing – some industries have significant barriers to sharing information between themselves.

Board members can be a very good information sharing resource, exchanging high level information and best practices across multiple organizations.

Improving information sharing between cooperating lawful organizations globally will help reduce the overall threat in the future.

I recommend using and understanding the automated exchange standards that are being developed by commercial entities, standards organizations and government agencies. Real time notification and defenses will be an important part of your future.

The board and C-Suite should drive the sharing initiative; insuring sharing is accomplished within multiple parts of the organization. This is not something you should leave only to IT.

Chapter 7: Government Activities in Cyber

"The greatest advances of civilization, whether in architecture or painting, in science and literature, in industry or agriculture, have never come from centralized government." - Milton Friedman

I could write an entire book on the inactivity and activity of the U.S. Federal Government in the cyber security domain, but will try to condense it down to the essentials in a few pages, and also address some new initiatives in the future direction chapter.

> *America must also face the rapidly growing threat from cyber-attacks. We know hackers steal people's identities and infiltrate private e-mail. We know foreign countries and companies swipe our corporate secrets. Now our enemies are also seeking the ability to sabotage our power grid, our financial institutions, and our air traffic control systems. We cannot look back years from now and wonder why we did nothing in the face of real threats to our security and our economy.*
>
> *That's why, earlier today, I signed a new executive order that will strengthen our cyber defenses by increasing information sharing, and developing standards to protect our national security, our jobs, and our privacy. Now, Congress must act as well, by passing legislation to give our government a greater capacity to secure our networks and deter attacks.*
>
> - President Obama, February 12, 2013

The U.S. Congress, known and unloved by most Americans these days by any statistical and polled measurement, has failed to pass any legislation concerning cyber security since 2002, according to the Congressional Research Center. Whatever your political leaning may be, this is horrendous bipartisan performance, and in lieu of legislation by Congress, the Executive Branch has issued a largely suggestive and voluntary pair of Executive Orders (EOs) that have some good ideas on sharing information and building a best practices framework, but is totally short on execution and enforcement. There are new initiatives being drafted and proposed inside of Congress, but nothing concrete was coming to closure as 2013 wound to a close.

In my (admittedly cynical, see anecdote below) opinion, it will likely take a massive cyber incident with far-reaching consequences occurring before comprehensive legislation and workable policy is created and implemented by the U.S. federal government. There are still a large number of unaddressed or poorly addressed items from the 9/11 commission as we approach the 13-year anniversary of those devastating attacks. Sadly, there are always many excuses and barriers to getting anything done.

Anecdote – Controlled Unclassified Information (CUI): On May 7, 2008, George Bush's Executive Office released an executive order on sharing information that was sensitive, but not classified and requiring a security clearance. This was an imperative issue that came out of the 9/11 Commission. The Federal Government had over 100 different ways of classifying information that was sensitive; in some cases using the same designation (e.g. SBU for Sensitive but Unclassified) with different rules depending on the civilian agency releasing the information. This could result in a large city mayor getting three documents from the federal agencies all designated SBU, but with completely different sharing restrictions. The Bush order was for a single, federal government-wide designation called Controlled Unclassified Information (CUI) and it made an immense amount of sense in terms of reducing confusion/cost and streamlining sharing between public and private entities. The National Archives was appointed as the lead agency to implement this simple, but powerful, construct. The Obama administration was elected and did a review that confirmed that this was a good course of action. Six years later, virtually nothing has happened on this simple but effective program that would have brought benefits far outweighing the costs. Millions expended, nothing changed.

This legislative gridlock and lack of agency response does not mean that individuals in the federal government are unaware of the risks from cyber – dire warnings have been voiced by several top agency heads. I've met many smart and committed people working the problems every day despite the lack of leadership and action at the top levels of government. Here are some relevant quotes from a subset of our U.S. government:

Director of National Intelligence James Clapper: "Cyber threats put all sectors of our country at risk, from government and private networks to critical infrastructures."

Defense Secretary Leon E. Panetta posited that the United States was facing the possibility of a "cyber-Pearl Harbor" and was increasingly vulnerable to foreign computer hackers who could dismantle the nation's power grid, transportation system, financial networks and government.

Senator Jay Rockefeller: In a letter to the Chairman of the Securities and Exchange Commission from five U.S. senators, including Commerce committee Chairman Jay Rockefeller, the Senators noted: "Every day, malicious actors attack and disrupt computer networks to steal valuable trade secrets, intellectual property, and financial and confidential information, causing significant damage to the United States Government, our citizens, our business, and our country."

Outgoing DHS secretary Janet Napolitano: "A massive and serious cyber-attack on the U.S. homeland is coming." Thanks for the parting optimism, Janet.

Senior Senator from Oregon Ron Wyden takes a much more complex view, "It is a fundamental principle of cyber-security that any network whose failure could result in loss of life or significant property should be physically isolated from the Internet," he said. "Unfortunately many of our critical network operators have violated this principle in order to save money or streamline operations. This sort of gross negligence should be the first target in any cyber-security program – not the privacy of individual Americans." (I disagree with his fundamental principal assertion – I think connectivity is inevitable and an armadillo approach will not stand the test of time, but I do feel that enhanced critical infrastructure protection is vital to our national security).

Former Secretary of Defense Robert Gates: "The only defense the United States has against nation states and other potential threats in the cyber world is the National Security Agency," he said. "You cannot replicate the National Security Agency for domestic affairs. There isn't enough money, there isn't enough time, and there isn't enough human talent."

The Federal government is also spending aggressively on cyber defenses and offensive capabilities – using cyber as one of our weapons in the event of a conflict. Spending in 2013 was estimated by NDIA (National Defense Industrial Association) at over $10 billion across the federal government and projected to increase by more than 6% per year for the next several years.

Ten federal programs alone represent more than $6.6 billion in cyber spending in 2013, and this is one area where spending will likely increase instead of decrease in the coming years.

- DISA – Defense Enterprise Computing Centers
- DISA – Global Command and Control System
- Army – Warfighter Information Network – Tactical
- Army – Network Enterprise Technology Command
- Navy – Consolidated Afloat Networks Enterprise Service
- Navy – Next Generation Enterprise Network
- Air Force – Base Level Communications Infrastructure
- Air Force – Air and Space Operations Center
- Medical Health System – Electronic Health Record Way Ahead
- Medical Health System – MHS Cyber-infrastructure Services

In September 2012, West Virginia Senator Jay Rockefeller sent a letter to all Fortune 500 CEOs about cyber security, asking eight fundamental questions:

1. Has your company adopted a set of best practices to address its own cyber security needs?

2. If so, how were these cyber security practices developed?

3. Were they developed by the company solely, or were they developed outside the company? If developed outside the company, please list the institution, association, or entity that developed them.

4. When were these cyber security practices developed? How frequently have they been updated? Does your company's board of directors or audit committee keep abreast of developments regarding the development and implementation of these practices?

5. Has the federal government played any role, whether advisory or otherwise, in the development of these cyber security practices?

6. What are your concerns, if any, with a voluntary program that enables the federal government and the private sector to develop, in coordination, best cyber security practices for companies to adopt as they so choose, as outlined in the Cybersecurity Act of 2012?

7. What are your concerns, if any, with the federal government conducting risk assessments, in coordination with the private sector, to best understand where our nation's cyber vulnerabilities are, as outlined in the Cybersecurity Act of 2012?

8. What are your concerns, if any, with the federal government determining, in coordination with the private sector,

the country's most critical cyber infrastructure, as outlined in the Cybersecurity Act of 2012?

Senator Rockefeller references the Cybersecurity Act of 2012, which was a piece of legislation proposed by Senators Joe Lieberman (I-CT) and Susan Collins (R-ME), but blocked from proceeding in the Senate in late 2012. The bill had language that would have bolstered critical infrastructure protections and information sharing, along with many other key areas of concern. President Obama, frustrated with the congressional debate, then issued an executive order on cyber and critical infrastructure that is contained in full in the Appendix, but can be summarized as follows:

Executive Order (EO) 13636, "Improving Critical Infrastructure Cybersecurity:"

Date: February 19, 2013

Key elements:

- **Development of a cybersecurity framework:** NIST (National Institute of Standards and Technology was given the task of producing this within 12 months of the issuance of the executive order. They have taken the task to heart and polled a large number of organizations for feedback. A preliminary framework has been published and can be found on the NIST website, with the final coming in early 2014 – potentially adjusted for the period of the government shutdown.

125

- **New information-sharing to provide classified and unclassified threat and attack information to U.S. companies:** DHS (Department of Homeland Security) is largely responsible for coordinating information-sharing with organizations, augmented by the DOD (Department of Defense) doing some excellent sharing programs with the DIB (Defense Industrial Base) – companies that are critical suppliers to our military. DHS will expand the classified sharing program to all sectors of critical infrastructure, and work to grant clearances to viable individuals in the private sector. They will also scale up their efforts to share more and to try to share in real time – since sending a notice of an attack once it is over is not going to help anyone. The real time aspect is troubling for the federal government – DHS does a poor overall job with information dissemination with program like HSIN – the Homeland Security Information Network. The general feeling in industry is that CNN and other news stations generally deliver information hours ahead of the federal government. The one group I've worked with that does a great job is NOAA and National Weather Service, who delivers real time weather threats across a broad spectrum of individuals and organizations. Other agencies could learn a lot from NOAA, but it's unlikely to happen based on my experience.

- **A voluntary program to promote the adoption of the framework:** The executive order is based on voluntary compliance, though later legislation may hone in on the best practices and turn them into legislation. Voluntary self-regulation may be a good way to start down the path, since most organizations will adopt the ones that work for them. This vetting process through adoption and use can be very effective. DHS is tasked with the task of promoting the framework.

- **Review of existing cybersecurity regulation:** Our governmental structure has many areas where things are done on a decentralized basis – the Department of Agriculture may issue regulations that are completely different than the Department of Energy, despite the fact that commercial organizations may deal with both agencies. This is only at the federal level; when you add in the state and local regulations, you can get an incredible matrix of regulatory and compliance issues that you have to deal with. Streamlining and aligning the regulatory requirements makes a lot of sense.

- **Strong privacy and civil liberties protections based on the Fair Information Practice Principles:** The government is tasked with considering all the impact on privacy a comprehensive cyber defense might have on individual's information and rights to anonymity. There are plenty of watchdog groups keeping a close eye on this issue after the large scale exposure of NSA programs involving surveillance.

While the executive order is aimed at critical infrastructure, there is nothing precluding other organizations from adopting the best practices resulting from the bill. NIST had several open sessions for input and feedback, and invited a broad segment of participants to discuss how all the different framework elements could help everyone achieve better cyber awareness and defenses. Information sharing will help all if it can be accomplished in real time and at multiple levels of sharing. It's not clear whether the federal government can step up and execute.

Federal Law Enforcement: The Department of Justice has an active set of initiatives to try to stem the tide of attacks and bring the attackers to justice. The FBI has reorganized and moved a significant number of resources into a cyber-security task force that works at both the international, national and state/local level. The FBI website puts the resource level they are committing as hundreds of agents, and the agency has achieved a significant number of prosecutions of high profile cyber criminals.

State/Local Intelligence Fusion Centers: The fusion centers were an outgrowth of the response to the 9/11 attacks on the World Trade Center and the Pentagon. The issue of "connecting the dots" caused a reorganization of the intelligence community as well, but one of the real issues was the difficult linkage between the different elements in the homeland security space, often termed FSLTIPP for Federal, State, Local, Tribal, International, Public and Private. The fusion centers are in just about every state, with multiple states having two centers because of their large populations, geographic disparity, or some recurring turf battles. These centers are designed to be the interface from state and local law enforcement to the federal law enforcement agencies, of which there are many – FBI, Park Police, Customs and Border Patrol, Secret Service, ATF (Alcohol, Tobacco, and Firearms) and several others. The centers are all different in terms of structure, funding, personnel and technology. Several had adopted a significant cyber security sharing effort and presented some of their best practices at the National Fusion Center Training Conference in 2013.

Attacks from within: During the same period of legislative inactivity around cyber, the U.S. Federal Government experienced two highly publicized events that compromised vast amounts of classified information. Both Bradley Manning, as an active duty serviceman and Edward Snowden, as a highly-cleared Booz Allen contractor working for the NSA, downloaded and publicized copious amounts of Secret and Top Secret information. On a *60 Minutes* interview, Michael Morrell, who served with the CIA for

33 years, identified the Edward Snowden breach as the most serious incident in the history of the government classified material use. The impact on the Snowden data breach is still evolving, with a recent bombshell that hinted at collusion between the NSA and one of the top cybersecurity companies, RSA. There will be entire books written that will analyze the breach impact. There is an emerging debate over whether Snowden is a traitor or a hero, with very strong positions being taken by both sides of the discussion. The short lesson to learn in our context is that insiders can do a significant amount of damage if they are not monitored and constrained.

NSA impact: The information that Edward Snowden released about National Security Agency programs has been headline news around the world. Countries are incensed about eavesdropping, U.S. citizens are irate about personal data collection, and technology companies are concerned about many different security aspects. The result is a distinct cooling of attitudes of cooperation and has raised defenses resulting from suspicions that there are more bombshells on the way. The ultimate result of these disclosures may be a decrease in sharing and openness, which will be unfortunate for defensive efforts for all concerned. Our government leadership has to step up and take control of these very intricate and involved issues, insuring that we are creating a climate of cooperation on security without unbalancing the rights of the people.

DHS CDM (Continuous Diagnostic and Mitigation): The Department of Homeland Security has recently released a major program aimed at protecting and fortifying all federal websites against cyber-attacks. DHS will also work with state and local governments and the defense industrial base sector of critical infrastructure. The idea is to deploy an array of sensors across all the networks and drive useful and real time information into the hands of network administrators. DHS has allocated up to six billion dollars under an IDIQ (Indefinite Delivery Indefinite Quantity) contract awarded to multiple firms – allowing DHS to pick and choose technology and suppliers based on task orders and requirements from the various constituents. This is a big investment and hopefully will fund strong development of tools, services and processes that can also be offered to critical infrastructure sectors and other organizations as well. There will likely be spotty participation by other federal partners as agencies have a history of going their own ways and not leveraging the lessons of their counterparts.

Globally, there are many countries paying attention to the cyber threat and several global consortiums that are working various parts of the cyber security terrain:

INTERPOL: INTERPOL is a well-established International Law Enforcement entity that helps span the jurisdictional issues across countries. It has a large number of member countries and had been doing significant information sharing for many years, helping to track down criminals of all types across the continents. INTERPOL announced in 2012 that they will be building a dedicated cyber security center in Singapore and that cyber will become part of their ongoing mission.

ENISA: The Europeans are taking cyber security very seriously and have more extensive data protection policies than the rest of the world. In order to combine their efforts, the member countries have created a European agency empowered to act. The consortium creates many research reports and advocates high payoff initiatives like information sharing, and several pointers to their work can be found in the resource section of this work.

From the ENISA site: "The European Union Agency for Network and Information Security (ENISA) is a center of network and information security expertise for the EU, its Member States, the private sector and Europe's citizens. ENISA works with these groups to develop advice and recommendations on good practice in information security. It assists EU Member States in implementing relevant EU legislation and works to improve the resilience of Europe's critical information infrastructure and networks. ENISA seeks to enhance existing expertise in EU Member States by supporting the development of cross-border communities committed to improving network and information security throughout the EU." More information about ENISA and its work can be found at www.enisa.europa.eu

United Nations: The United Nations convened its third cyber security summit in Seoul, South Korea in October of 2013. Eighty-seven countries sent representatives and this was the first cyber conference where developing nations were invited to attend. A wide range of topics were discussed including how to build enhanced trust and confidence worldwide. Coordination and collaboration by nations of all types was deemed necessary and an emphasis on prevention versus response was also encouraged. The outcomes report is listed in the resources section. The next meeting of this type will take place in 2015, likely in the Netherlands.

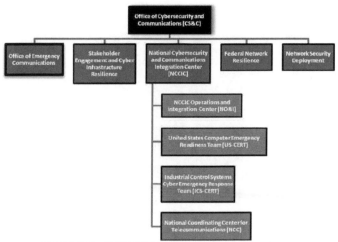

SOURCE: DHS IG Report dated October 2

Chapter 7 Key Points Summary:

Governments around the world have embraced cyber security as a major threat/risk.

Significant effort has been made to highlight the problem and build collaboration with the private sector. Much of it is not working.

The U.S. government is spending aggressively on its own cyber defense and offense capabilities.

There are cyber efforts underway in many different sections of government, sometimes overlapping and conflicting. Compare and contrast your different sources.

The U.S. government is doing little real-time unclassified cyber information sharing in the cyber space. NOAA can notify people of tornadoes in real time, but DHS and DOJ are lagging on this vital initiative.

The U.S. government has irritated and caused a rift in cooperation between many of our allies with the accusations of spying on world leaders by the NSA. This may reduce the amount of sharing until the situation stabilizes.

Use your organization's capabilities to influence our elected officials to action versus rhetoric.

Chapter 8: Cyber Information Resources

"We are drowning in information, while starving for wisdom. The world henceforth will be run by synthesizers, people able to put together the right information at the right time, think critically about it, and make important choices wisely." - E. O. Wilson, American Biologist

The cyber security world is a swirling sea of changes that occur on a minute by minute basis. The November 2013 issue of *CSO*, a magazine devoted to the Chief Security Officer, ran an article about cybersecurity not becoming a "profession" until it stops changing so fast. The article contrasts the mostly self-taught cyber responders with a professionalized career path based on a fairly static set of knowledge that can be measured, certified, and tested on a recurring basis.

Until this type of industry stabilization takes place, which could be a decade away, it will be important to stay current with industry changes, maintaining a continual situational or cyber-intelligence awareness picture. In this chapter, I have tried to identify as many of the resources available that provide information, alerts, research papers and other valuable news about the emerging threat picture. The good news is that many organizations and product/service vendors expend great effort into publishing useful information, and most of the information is made publically available. Because there is so much, finding ways to harness what is important for your organization is critical.

There are sources that address the global market and others that are specifically focused on an industry segment or attack type. In today's world of almost instantaneous publishing, your first instinct should be to research what others have already communicated. It may save you time on your planning or response and give you a broader view of the issue. I've used Google Alerts for years to monitor a set of different topics – one set of keywords delivers a daily digest of news around that defined subject.

The power of collaboration: Sharing relevant, specific articles across an organization can pay substantial dividends in terms of coverage and time saving. Read, comment, highlight, draw parallels to a specific internal issue and get it to others via SharePoint, email, internal RSS feed or any of the many other tools you likely already have in place. The cumulative time wasted across large organizations reading the same things is astonishing to me. Work to leverage the time spent wherever possible.

Multi-sourcing – expand your horizons: Many of the people reading this will come from an era where reading text is the de facto standard for information transmission. I would encourage you to expand your horizons and look for new sources that can provide diversity and different learning scenarios. YouTube has a library of video that is updated daily and the content can be far more useful than the trending viral cat video – many conferences will post sessions and individuals will create surprisingly high quality video lectures. Podcasts distributed mostly through Apple's iTUNES also are a fantastic resource for recurring experts in the field and can be consumed on the road and in the gym, stretching your effective time.

Source filtering: I've tried to orient the list to sites and sources useful by the readers of this book – board members, executive leadership and less technical individuals concerned about the organization's cyber posture and hygiene. There are thousands of sources in many different areas when you include sites that are oriented to the technical professionals that will be staffing your organization's defenses. Many of those sites are also useful for the attackers when a new vulnerability is announced. You may be targeted if you don't take rapid action to close that hole in your defenses.

Assume all the websites I've listed are freely available. I will do a separate section on sites that require payment or subscriptions. Many of the free websites will have additional member only areas or paid services.

Reporting incidents/suspicious activity: If you encounter an attack or breach and you decide to report it (which you should under almost all circumstances), these are some of the major reporting sites:

- **United States**: www.us-cert.gov US-CERT is a division of the Department of Homeland Security and is a tremendous resource for cyber security information. You can report incidents to DHS and also sign up for alerts from their feed.

- **Europe:** www.europol.europa.eu/content/report-cybercrime-online Europol provides an overall set of links to different countries for reporting cybercrime and incidents. See below for the list of countries addressed.

- **Australia:** www.asd.gov.au/infosec/reportincident.htm The Australian Signals Directorate has an Adobe PDF form that you can download and submit, as well as phone numbers where you can call.

SOURCE: Europol website

My top recommended informational websites are below. I did not put them in a priority or alphabetical order, so don't read anything into the sequence in which they appear:

- **SANS Institute:** www.sans.org   SANS is one of the premier organizations in the cybersecurity world and they provide a wealth of information and training. Their top 20 security controls are widely used, and very well thought out.

- **CIO/CSO:** www.cio.com, www.csoonline.com are two of the global brands for IDG (International Data Group) in Framingham, MA. These sites cover an immense amount of the information systems arena, and provide very good cybersecurity coverage. They are aimed mainly at the Chief Information Officer and Chief Security Officer positions, but typically have well thought-out materials that anyone can absorb.

- **Ponemon Institute:** www.ponemon.org This organization puts out several significant research papers that are very readable and aggregate much of the threat picture across a wide range of companies.

- **CYLAB (Carnegie Mellon):** https://www.cylab.cmu.edu/ CYLAB is the largest and one of the most respected university programs focused on cyber security. CYLAB positions itself as a resource that brings other resources together into a unified effort that crosses public and private boundaries.

- **Darkreading.com:** www.darkreading.com This site is pretty technical, but has some very good summary information and is quick to report emerging threats. They have easy to understand slideshows that can be useful for non-technical viewers.

- **RSA:** www.rsa.com RSA, a division of EMC, is one of the global leaders in security, and there is wealth of information at their sites. I'd highly recommend their conferences as well, and they have been taking a forward-leaning view toward information sharing through their MILE initiative.

- **Mandiant:** www.mandiant.com Mandiant was acquired by FireEye in a billion dollar transaction announced in early 2014. Mandiant is one of the world leaders in forensics and attack detection, and was credited with the discovery of a Chinese military group doing extensive cyber exploration around the world.

- **Microsoft:** www.microsoft.com Microsoft is one of the most embedded companies in the cyber defense world. Their software runs the majority of the world's computers and their Azure Cloud is one of the leading contenders for dominance. They have a Trustworthy Computing initiative and offer a wide range of cyber information. They also offer a set of vulnerability patches on a regular basis, allowing system administrators to keep their systems current and up to date.

- **IBM:** www.ibm.com Microsoft has the volume, but IBM equipment hosts a huge amount of the world's business transactions on legacy mainframe applications in banking, transportation, retail, energy and other critical industries. IBM issues some very good industry reports through their Global Services arm.

- **Dell SecureWorks:** www.secureworks.com Dell's SecureWorks is a leading provider of managed services in the cyber defense market and also provides a wealth of information around cyber threats.

- **Online Trust Alliance:** www.otalliance.org As the name implies, OTA is focused on a broad mission around trust, privacy, security and identity. They are a nonprofit organization and offer membership to participate. They offer very good information and reports about the cyber world's ongoing challenges.

- **OWASP:** www.owasp.org The Open Web Application Security Project has a mission to make software more secure around the world. OWASP is another global nonprofit that harnesses the efforts of many into some concrete steps toward a more secure future.

- **ZDNET:** www.zdnet.com/blog/security ZDNET is one of the perennial media companies covering the computer industry. Their "Zero Day" security blog covers many current topics and new threats.

- **Information Week:** www.informationweek.com/security.asp The Information Week website offers a broad range of articles on the business computing environment and cyber landscape.

Consulting and response services: This list is a definite subset of all the firms out there offering consulting and response services. I have either worked with them directly or have direct exposure to them through clients that I have done work for. If your firm offers something unique, contact me and I'll add you to subsequent versions of the e-book.

- **Mandiant:** Mandiant www.mandiant.com is one of the premier response companies in the cyber security space. The company recently became part of FireEye and the combined entities should create more preventative and mitigation products and services. Mandiant has done the world a favor by releasing their OPEN-IOC framework (Indicators of Compromise) to the public domain to spur automated exchange of real time information.

- **Levick:** Levick (www.levick.com) is a crisis public relations firm that is very adept at helping organizations handle the communications response needed in the event of a major cyber-attack. As noted in the preparedness chapter, engaging firms like this proactively versus reactively will result in a better level of service and overall response.

- **Dell SecureWorks:** Secure Works www.secureworks.com provides a continuous set of services for monitoring and diagnosing systems and networks and has come highly recommended by several Chief Information Officers that I have worked with.

- **PWC:** PwC (formerly Price Waterhouse Coopers) www.pwc.com is a powerhouse of a consulting firm with 180,000 employees worldwide. They have people in all aspects of risk, governance, audit, and a growing cybersecurity capability.

- **Deloitte:** Deloitte (www.deloitte.com) is one of the largest global consulting firms and has a substantial cyber security practice.

- **EY:** EY (Ernst and Young) www.ey.com covers 140 countries around the world with their global efforts and like PwC and Deloitte, can provide a wealth of services across most large corporation's needs.

- **RSA:** RSA (www.rsa.com) is owned by EMC (www.emc.com) and has been one of the perennial cyber security powerhouses in the industry. Their conference is always sold out and they have a wide range of products and services. They are one of the companies at the forefront of automated information sharing.

- **IBM:** IBM's global services group (www.ibm.com) is the world's largest business and technology service provider, covering the entire world with an army of personnel.

U.S. government sites you may find useful: These government sites have extensive information and most have a good search feature for finding the documents and web pages you want to see. Insure that you are cross-checking information for age, redundancy and conflicts across agencies - the connectivity of the Internet has not solved the information silo challenges within our bureaucracy:

- **Department of Homeland Security**: www.dhs.gov
- **US-CERT:** www.us-cert.gov/
- **Executive Branch:** www.whitehouse.gov
- **Department of Justice:** www.fbi.gov
- **National Institute of Standards and Technology:** www.nist.gov
- **Department of Transportation:** www.dot.gov
- **Department of Energy**: www.doe.gov
- **Federal Trade Commission**: www.ftc.gov
- **Federal Communications Commission:** www.fcc.gov
- **Office of the Director of National Intelligence:** www.odni.gov
- **Department of Defense**: www.dod.gov

Organizations:

- **U.S. Chamber of Commerce:** www.uschamber.com The Chamber is all about the private sector and represents a large number on many different areas of legislation and interface to the federal government.

- **Business Roundtable**: www.businessroundtable.org The Business Roundtable is an association of Chief Executive Officers that represent many of the largest companies in the United States in terms of shaping public policy.

- **INFRAGARD:** www.infraguard.org Sponsored by the FBI as a public/private partnership, there are INRAGARD chapters in most major cities that provide briefings and highlight threats.

- **NACD (National Association of Corporate Directors):** www.nacdonline.com NACD is an association centered on educating and building improved governance and board of directors in all types of organizations.

Reports used during the research portion of this book that were particularly insightful or useful:

- Ponemon Institute 2013 Cost of Cyber Report: http://www.ponemon.org/library/2012-cost-of-cyber-crime-study

- OTA 2013 Data Protection and Breach Readiness Report: https://otalliance.org/resources/Incident.html

- IBM Security Services Cyber Security Intelligence Index: http://public.dhe.ibm.com/common/ssi/ecm/en/sew03031us en/SEW03031USEN.PDF

- FireEye, The Need for Speed:2013 Incident Response Survey: http://docs.ismgcorp.com/files/handbooks/Incident-Response-Survey-2013/fireeye_Incident_response_survey_report.pdf

- Carnegie Mellon CYLAB 2012 report on enterprise security: http://globalcyberrisk.com/wp-content/uploads/2012/08/CMU-GOVERNANCE-RPT-2012-FINAL1.pdf

- PwC: Defending Yesterday: Key Findings from the Global State of Information Security Survey 2014: http://www.pwc.com/et_EE/EE/publications/assets/pub/gsiss-2014.pdf

- SANS Security Analytics Survey September 2013: https://www.sans.org/reading-room/analysts-program/security-analytics-survey-2013

- GTRI Emerging Cyber Threats Report 2014: http://www.gtcybersecuritysummit.com/2014Report.pdf

- EY European Audit Committee Leadership Network ViewPoints: http://www.ey.com/Publication/vwLUAssets/Cyber_securit

y_and_the_board/$FILE/ViewPoints%2033-%20Cybersecurity%20-16%20January%202013.pdf

- Dell Secure Works: Incident Response and Digital Forensics: http://www.secureworks.com/incident-response/

- Verizon White Paper: Verizon Enterprise Risk and Incident Sharing Metrics Framework: http://www.verizonenterprise.com/resources/whitepapers/wp_verizon-incident-sharing-metrics-framework_en_xg.pdf

- Verizon 2013 Data Breach Investigations Report: http://www.verizonenterprise.com/DBIR/2013/

- Executive Branch: National Strategy for Information Sharing and Safeguarding December 2012: http://www.whitehouse.gov/sites/default/files/docs/2012sharingstrategy_1.pdf

- Microsoft security blog: http://blogs.technet.com/b/security/

- United Nations 2013 Seoul Cyber Security Conference: www.seoulcyber2013.kr/admin/board/downJaryoFile.do?jaryo_id=461&atch_file_id=${list.atch_file_id}

Chapter 8 Key Points Summary:

There are thousands of sources of cyber information across the globe. Most are freely available.

The publish rate of new articles, white papers, videos and vendor information is very high, so a strategy for staying current is a good defensive step and worth the investment.

Building a network of people who screen and forward good information as they find it can save time and ensure a broader coverage of the issues.

The publish date on any given piece of material is important – something from 2005 may be largely useless or outdated in today's threat environment.

Look for industry specific sources – beyond the immediate information, you will learn who the thought leaders in your segment are considered to be, and who is most active in terms of sharing.

Conferences can provide invaluable information and introductions – ensure that you are sending the right level person to the right conferences. Share the results broadly.

YouTube.com has many conferences and other presentations on cyber security that you can watch if you are a more visual learner or can't dedicate the time to full conference attendance.

Very good information is published by groups outside the technical IT space: lawyers, consultants and other professional groups. Ensure that you are consuming a broad range of opinions within your organization.

Chapter 9: A Standardized Approach for Your Efforts

"If I have seen further than others, it is by standing upon the shoulders of giants." - Isaac Newton

This chapter might seem a little out of place – while I have tried to approach the cyber issues at a high level, this information will take you up another 20,000 feet, giving you an even broader perspective of an approach that could be very useful in organizing your efforts. There are some valuable lessons from the physical and digital world that can help with framing the future of consistent, repeatable and interoperable cyber defenses.

Silver Bullets: How Interoperable Data will Revolutionize Information Sharing: I published this book in 2010 (available through Amazon and other bookstores that might still exist) and many of the key principals of data interoperability hold true in the cyber realm. In the chapter on cyber information sharing, we looked at some of the initiatives that were underway to automate and standardize cyber information at many different levels. This chapter attempts to make you think outside the cyber world, and visualize a long term, repeatable solution that would move this problem to a more manageable set of processes that can be repeated and built upon. While cyber is a unique risk, processes can be standardized and replicated for the activities around attacks and response, saving you time and dollars.

I've tried to relate a standardized data approach to things you will intuitively understand rather than a jumble of technical identifiers – explaining detailed standards like ISO 27001 and IEC 27002 are beyond the scope of this book in terms of detail, and likely your level of interest. The lesson to learn is that properly applied, standardized information can greatly streamline a process and allow interoperability across your organization and those you choose to share with.

Standards have been vital to civilizations moving forward and building on past results. Take a quick trip through history and see for yourself how standardized physical technology helped position the world for the digital revolution:

Weight and measures: When was the last time that you paid attention to whether something you bought was weighed or measured correctly? As soon as mankind started trading salt for shells and cloth for gold pieces, coming to an agreement on "how much" for "how many" became important. And once structures evolved past rude huts, standardized measurements of distance became necessary.

Early measurements were variable. A foot could vary by as much as three to four inches; a yard was the distance from the tip of the nose to the end of an outstretched arm. Cubits, spans, and other approximate distances made up the world of measurement for thousands of years. Weight was just as variable. The Babylonians used various standardized stones for different categories of weight; the butcher, horseman, wool-seller or fishmonger might each use stones of different weights. The Egyptians and Greeks used the wheat seed as their smallest unit of weight. The Arabs used a small bean called a carob as a means to weigh precious jewels; this standard has evolved into the "carat" used for diamonds and other gems.

The Romans inevitably intermixed many of these early standards as their empire grew and expanded over much of the known world. Being able to understand and discuss long distances became important, and scaled maps began to evolve. When the Roman Empire collapsed and Europe drifted into the Dark Ages, innovation in this area (as in so many others) was squelched. Sometime after the Magna Carta was signed, King Edward I of England set a permanent standard for the yard, which is very close to today's standard. England later revised the yard based on a uniform pendulum measurement.

Much later, in 1793, Napoleonic French scientists invented the metric system, which used the decimal system and brought order to the world of weights and measures. It was based on the meter – with 10 million meters representing the distance from the Equator to the North Pole – a scientific measurement that could be validated. (After 17 years of implementation, France dropped the metric system, then returned to it for good in 1837.) Other standards followed, but adjustments in both metric and Imperial (feet-and-inches) systems continued. As recently as 1959, the length of the International Yard and the International Foot were agreed on in the U.S. and Commonwealth countries. The new lengths were shorter than the previous U.S. definition and longer than the previous U.K. definition.

Today, the modern metric system is used almost worldwide, with the United States as the major exception. The U.S. toyed with the idea of adopting the metric system since before France adopted it the first time – Thomas Jefferson did a report calling for an advanced set of weights and measures in 1790. John Quincy Adams did another report in 1821, as America watched the rest of the world move toward the metric system. I remember learning the metric system in 1967 (fifth grade) and being told that the U.S. was going to convert. I don't know the reason for the conversion failure, but suspect early lobbyists and special interests.

Interchangeable parts: Eli Whitney was one of America's foremost inventors. He transformed the cotton industry in the southern United States by developing the cotton "gin" (short for "engine"), which could automatically separate seeds from the white fibers that had come into huge demand worldwide – increasing production and speed to market dramatically. This had previously been a time-consuming, labor-intensive process. Regrettably, the design of the cotton gin was very simple and repeatable, which was a huge frustration for Whitney. Despite the patent he was granted for his device, everyone copied his design at will, causing him to move north to Washington D.C.

Eli's real contribution to interoperability came after he returned north. At this period in time every gun was crafted by hand, limiting the size and scale of the military forces. Eli received a contract from the government to produce 1,000 muskets from interchangeable parts – an attempt to circumvent the bottleneck that limited the production of firearms to the number of qualified gunsmiths. History shows that Eli accomplished his goal, and that interchangeable part manufacturing's vision was ratified. Parts from one firearm could be interchanged with parts from a like firearm – a major accomplishment that allowed a significant increase in manufacturing capabilities of new rifles, and, just as importantly, facilitated field maintenance and the combination of parts when necessary.

I heard a follow-on comment to Eli's genius at a lecture about object-oriented programming in Sausalito, California. After much hard work and experimentation under his government contract, Eli was apparently over budget and behind schedule, and as a result, the government was going to cancel his contact, bankrupting his company. The story goes that in recent times, someone went back to the original parts that were still in the Smithsonian and discovered microscopic file marks – Eli had faked the demonstration!!

Eli Whitney's technology later achieved very large scale at Harper's Ferry Armory; site of John Brown's uprising in 1859. The armory's mass production techniques (interoperable standards at work) were so impressive that Robert E. Lee, commander of the Union forces that put down the John Brown uprising, made it one of his first priorities to capture and move the technology south when Virginia and other states seceded and formed the Confederacy – enlisting Lee as their commander.

7.62mm NATO ammunition: The history behind the development of this standardized ammunition could fill an entire book. For our purposes, think about seven different men from seven different countries in a World War I foxhole, each with a different rifle and a different type of proprietary ammunition. No matter what happens, there is no interoperability between them – if one has 5,000 bullets, it does none of the others any good. When NATO standardized on the 7.62mm cartridge, suddenly everyone could make guns and bullets that worked together – a German gun could shoot French bullets, an American rifle could load Italian-made ammo, and interoperability was achieved.

I've been told that the Russians designed their 7.62mm cartridge just a bit bigger than NATO's so that Soviet bloc countries received two standardized advantages: interoperability between Soviet Bloc manufacturers, and the added bonus of using NATO ammunition without reciprocating that capability to the NATO Alliance. The slightly larger cartridge would jam NATO rifles, but the Soviets could use either – making captured ammunition a real prize!

Shipping containers: As a child, I went to a replica of a colonial village somewhere in New York State. Beyond the butter churning demonstration, the hog pit, and other depictions of frontier life, was a ship at the docks. Dock workers rolled barrels, lifted boxes, and carried crates on and off of the ship – all for show, but it made the point. This laborious "break bulk" process – hand loading and unloading of ships – was prone to damage, errors, and shrinkage. It continued until 1956, when shipping started slowly moving to an interoperable standard that changed the civilized world as we know it: the uniform industry shipping container that has standardized to a metal box 40 feet long by 8 feet wide by 8½ feet high.

Malcolm McLean sent the first 58 containers from New Jersey to Texas, initiating one of the biggest industrial changes the world had experienced. In less than 40 years, dockworker productivity increased by over a factor of 8,000, and seaports rose and fell in importance based on their adoption of this rapidly emerging new standard. Ships were subsequently built around the container standard, allowing ship speeds to increase, while prices for international movement of goods decreased dramatically. An entire industry grew up around the container business – loaders, truck beds, and innumerable other devices were needed – all built around the basic shipping container standard. Interoperability with the trucking industry helped the railroads flourish.

Why did it take so long to figure this out, when this seems so apparent in hindsight? What an amazing transition, all in a relatively short period of time. A triumph of standardization and interoperability!

The digital world was born with the introduction of large scale, special purpose computers funded for the World War II effort. These behemoths ran with primitive circuitry and used an immense amount of space and other resources like air conditioning and electricity. The transistor was first invented in 1947, laying the groundwork for an entire generation of new technology. Here are some of the standards that moved this early digital age into the mainstream that we know today:

COBOL: When computers were first developed, programming these behemoths was a task for very sophisticated individuals with deep math and engineering backgrounds. Much of the early work was done in binary machine language (literally typing 1s and 0s, or flipping binary switches on complicated control panels) and assembly language (one step advanced, but still very close to the machine architecture). Early applications were impressive (for the time). As an example, calculating artillery trajectory tables (which took weeks to do by hand with slide rules) could be accomplished in seconds – a huge time-saving application.

Rear Admiral Grace Hopper, a legendary computer scientist and Navy officer, developed a more English-like programming language called Flow-Matic. The Conference on Data Systems Languages (CODASYL), an industry consortium devoted to developing a standardized computing language, took Flow-Matic and turned the best of it, with other innovations, into the Common Business Oriented Language (COBOL). COBOL was adopted and became the basis for many millions of lines of computer code worldwide with acceptance driven by IBM and other computer manufacturing companies.

COBOL was so long-lasting that in the run-up to the year 2000, when I needed a COBOL expert to help prepare my company's networked system for potential changes and problems, I couldn't find anyone to hire; there just weren't enough people still working who knew the language. I ended up contracting with a couple of programmers living in a retirement home in New Jersey – the language had outlived many of its developers!

COBOL was one of the first open-standard, interoperable programming languages that could work on different computers. While it never achieved true portability (computer vendors always found a way to add small extensions and proprietary items to their compilers in the effort to lock customers in), it was close, and set the stage for many innovations in the business and computing world.

The IBM PC, MS-DOS, and Windows: When the IBM personal computer (PC) burst into being in 1981, it was a defining moment for the computer industry and had impact around the world. What most people don't remember is that there was already a plethora of PCs and operating systems available at the time – the Apple II, Tandy's (Radio Shack) TRS 80, CPM machines, and the Xerox

Star (which had most of the elements of the windows, icon, mouse, pointer [WIMP] interface initially popularized by the Apple Macintosh and years later by Microsoft Windows).

The IBM PC was a defining standard because IBM defied its own traditions and made it an open, standardized system. Within months of the IBM PC release, there were numerous compatible machines including the Compaq "luggable," a beast of a portable PC (at 28 lbs. and about $3,500) and a harbinger of what laptops would be. An entire industry standardized around Microsoft Disk Operating System (MS-DOS, released in 1982) and the open architecture – and millions upon millions of PCs were sold. Michael Dell built a billion dollar business out of the trunk of his car! Bill Gates had the vision to license MS-DOS to IBM and others on a per-copy basis instead of giving up all rights for a one-time development fee. This foresight resulted in his becoming the world's richest person. All this was due to the power of a standard – one that Microsoft happened to control, allowing the company to capture and hold nearly 100 percent market share for many years.

There were many lawsuits against Microsoft for monopolistic behavior, but imagine how much more slowly the industry would have developed if MS-DOS (and later, Windows) had not served as the central operating system for the hundreds of millions of PCs that evolved during the 1980s and 1990s. The standardized structure made it safer for organizations to make investments in technology, and encouraged developers to come up with new applications. A 5MB hard drive was massive for a short period of months, quickly replaced by a 10MB, then a 30MB, then ever-larger drives. New generations of standardized processors (built mostly by Intel Corporation) also set a new performance bar almost every 18 months – the 286, the 386, the 486, and then the Pentium. People talked about the specifications in great detail; clock speeds could and would be debated at cocktail parties. Today, much of the newness has worn off and few people know or care about the clock speed of their PC or Mac – the novel has become the commonplace.

The Internet took decades to develop, but reached its tipping point in the early nineties, and grew exponentially for many years after that. Tim Berners-Lee spearheaded the effort to create the information management system we now know as the World Wide Web, launched in 1991 – leveraging the infrastructure of the Internet, which was already far more developed. The WWW created a "web of hypertext documents," which could be linked to each other regardless of physical location. In 1993, the National Center for Supercomputing Applications (NCSA) launched the Mosaic web browser, and web use exploded. Marc Andreessen, leader of the Mosaic team at NCSA, started Netscape and released Netscape Navigator (which depended at least partly on standards established by Mosaic) in 1994. At its peak, Netscape accounted for 90% of all web browser use. Microsoft initiated the industry's first browser war by bundling Internet Explorer with Windows, and took over the browser market. As I write this, half a dozen browsers from other companies are challenging that dominance, including Google Chrome.

What many people also don't know or remember is that there were many standards working their way into the mainstream for years before the World Wide Web made Internet use commonplace: TCP/IP and DNS, to name just two. The Internet was built on the idea of interoperable data packets that could be disassembled, transported over various routes, and then magically re-assembled at the receiving location.

There were plenty of other networking protocols at the time – IBM had SNA (System Network Architecture) and if you were "true blue" (meaning every piece of your equipment was from IBM), you had a good chance at connecting everything together. Hewlett Packard and Digital Equipment Corporation both had networking protocols that connected their own equipment, but having multiple vendors' equipment on the same piece of cable or connected in the data center was a far leap. Many of the vendors disliked the idea of a unifying method for connecting – the fear (now realized in many environments) was that hardware would become a commodity, and cause the vendors to compete on price versus proprietary advantage.

As TCP/IP became a dominant standard (driven heavily by universities that couldn't afford separate networks or to go all-IBM), unified networks that could handle all types of computing equipment were increasingly favored. Proprietary standards were relegated to the back of the bus and ultimately consumed by a single, general purpose standard.

HTML: the lingua franca of the World Wide Web, was both a miracle and a curse of a standard – miraculous in that almost anyone could create these entities called web pages, and anyone with a browser and the correct Uniform Resource Locator (URL) could consume them from anywhere in the world regardless of the type of computer they used or network they were attached to. The curse was that the fairly immature standard took hold very quickly, and just as quickly ran into problems and irregularities that became harder to solve because of the rapidly expanding base of amateur programmers. There were tricks for each version of browser, and religious wars inside organizations fought over dumbing down the HTML or taking full advantage of proprietary techniques. Many of these issues have been solved, but there can be erratic behaviors on the same site when a different browser is used.

As civilization has advanced, we've built our world on standards that have emerged and become ingrained into our everyday lives As we move into subsequent chapters of our information age development, there will be many more cyber security standards that emerge and help make defending our systems more predictable, rigorous and automated.

Standardized solutions will eliminate some of the variability that plagues our current assortment of computing systems. The cloud environment is a technical greenfield where the technology deployed is not from the 1900's, so inherently newer and somewhat more standardized. Software development is the real challenge – despite some groundbreaking work by universities including Carnegie Mellon and MIT, much of our software is still cobbled together by smart people using primitive techniques. Standards are under development and emerging, but with the computer industry's relatively short tenure and continued rapid growth, building repeatable, secure components is still a major obstacle.

Chapter 9 Key Points Summary:

Standards have allowed civilization to develop large scale capabilities.

Creating a focus on using standardized approaches will pay dividends in the long term for your organization. The long term support costs go down greatly and capabilities increase.

Physical standards have existed for millennia, while our electronic computing capability is new to mankind in the last 60-70 years. We are still getting the hang of it and have a lot to learn.

Your organization should monitor and incorporate standardized approaches and interoperable information exchange formats for both internal and information sharing capabilities.

Automated, real time defense systems that will exchange information at machine speed across organizations will demand standards that will support comprehensive information transfer.

Standards, like technology, can be understood and managed by non-technical leadership if presented in a way where the function is emphasized. You want to focus on the water being delivered, leaving the pipes to the information plumbers.

Chapter 10: The Future of Cyber Security

"Any sufficiently advanced technology is indistinguishable from magic." - Arthur C. Clarke

The future of cyber security parallels the overall technology revolution and the continuing development of the Information Age that we've grown up with – the threat is expanding with every new capability brought to life. Where there is innovation in new services and technology, there is someone probing the new capability for weaknesses that can be exploited for entry, theft, disruption, or disablement. The primitive interconnections that exist between the many components of today's "sophisticated" enterprise systems only add to the increasing risk.

The risks from cyber-attacks will likely continue its rapid rise over the coming years – there are several new areas of growth that will open up major new attack vectors. Cloud computing, Software as a Service (SAAS), and the Internet of Things (IOT) are beginning or continuing to accelerate in terms of competitive advantage and cost reduction, and increased deployment brings new attack vectors. The new capabilities have their own inherent weaknesses, but the combination with existing systems magnifies these vulnerabilities.

Short term predictions for cyber threats – 2014 and 2015:

The Bad News: The number of attacks and the dollar impact of the attacks will continue to climb across our world. New threats will continue to emerge and the insider threat looms large. We are at risk of a major attack on our critical infrastructure by groups not motivated by stealing money, but by crippling the American economy. Nation-states will continue to probe each other, and there will significant activity in the intelligence community, shrouded by classification and need to know. Cyber criminals will continue to get smarter, taking advantage of information in the public domain and shared secretly. In addition to the current suite of attack methods already in place, here are some specific trends and predictions that will impact your organization:

- **Mobile/Smartphones:** There have not been any devastating attacks on the increasingly large base of mobile phones, but most research I have absorbed identifies this is an imminent area of risk. The result could have a major impact on what phone you are willing to use, and the current market leaders. A sophisticated insider attack on the iPhone infrastructure or code could leverage the rigid nature and relative standardization of all the proprietary Apple phones, enabling a wide spread security event. The Android mobile operating system, created by Google, is much more open, making its code an open book to attackers studying how to attack the users of this technology. Almost all phones have lax security, but there are also more limited ways to attack, and the information stored on most mobile phones has been less valuable than the server component of the enterprise. Insure that your organization is monitoring the mobile area for emerging threats – if a sophisticated attacker utilizes a mobile application as a bridge to break into larger systems, the problem becomes more pronounced.

- **Tablets:** Tablets are a growing threat and a larger risk to organizational infrastructure. Many people, particularly high level executives, are forgoing a traditional laptop and relying on a tablet for much of their day-to-day interaction with their organization, partners, and customers. This means those tablets are loaded with prizes for an attacker – confidential documents, contact databases, customer records, email repositories, and most of all, password files containing credentials to other systems. Despite the warnings and awareness building from the IT department, most senior employees and executives have a wide variety of access credentials, and because being senior many times is a product of getting older, those credentials are likely written down somewhere. Many people have a file that holds all the other passwords they have, and this file is an attack point. Your organization should continue to monitor this problem and insure that encryption is being used wherever feasible.

- **Ransomware:** Ransomware is a newer threat and is a significant, growing problem. The first attacks emerged out of Russia in 2005. The threat manifests through malware, and encrypts a portion of the user's storage so that it can't be used. The attacker demands a payment to unencrypt the information and release it to normal use. One highly effective version has been the Police Trojan – malware encrypts the information and send the user a message that the local police department suspects the computer involved in illegal activity and a fine must be paid to unlock it. From an organizational standpoint, there are a couple of big concerns here. First, this infection can be embarrassing and isolate the attacked user to using their personal credit card to avoid letting centralized IT know about the invasion. This interaction with an attacker could open the door to a larger attack – imagine you get a link to the decrypt code and you accept it – there is nothing to prevent a further malicious scan or download to your device that loads an even more malicious, hidden piece of malware to be activated later. There is also nothing to prevent the attacker from being able to reactivate the ransom software and continue the extortion multiple times.

If it is easier to deal with the hacker than with your internal IT group, you are setting the stage for a long term debacle.

- **Industrial Control Systems (ICS):**   Most industrial control systems were built as stand-alone, localized implementations. With the advent of the Internet and new generations of devices and control software, this has caused many isolated systems to be reachable via the internet or other intruder methods like USB-based software injection. There is an increasing likelihood that major attacks will occur, causing disruption or physical damage. If your organization utilizes these types of systems, it's imperative to fund preparedness and resilience efforts.

- **Cyber professionals:**   The creation of highly qualified, experienced cyber professionals at all levels will not meet the current and growing demand worldwide. There are many universities that have added cyber security and information security degree programs, and a host of certification-granting organizations has also emerged. Over time, this will help somewhat, but the experience factor is still an important element.   To mitigate this negative trend, organizations need to ensure that they have good people, contract with outside providers for surge resources, continually vet and validate internal resources and work with internal teams to align organizational strategy with resource expenditures and planning.

Potential Good News: While there are many areas for concern, and a continual set of emerging threats, there are several areas where the trends are positive:

- **The cyber market:**   Every new threat creates a corresponding demand for assistance and the global free market has been answering the call in the cyber security arena. Product sales have increased for existing vendors and new companies have been created to produce products and services to support the worldwide cyber defense and response market. A good example is FireEye, a Silicon Valley company that started in 2004 and recently executed an initial public offering based on some impressive global product sales. Even more recently, FireEye acquired Mandiant, arguably the premiere cyber response and forensics company based in Washington, D.C. There will continue to be a significant amount of capital invested worldwide into a broad variety of solutions, products, and service offerings.

- **Top level attention**: Senior management and the Board of Directors are paying an increased amount of attention to the risks presented by cyber threats. The National Association of Corporate Directors (www.nacdonline.org) has incorporated cyber into their "Master Classes" for board member development and also included speakers and panels into their annual meeting format. Audit and risk firms like PwC and Deloitte are also highlighting the importance of cyber preparedness as a top level risk for corporations. Increasing government discussions have pushed organizations like the Business Roundtable and Chamber of Commerce to drive initiatives around voluntary self-regulation.

- **Cyber information sharing:** Information sharing initiatives by government, industry, and non-profits will continue to gather momentum globally and begin to shorten the time frame from reporting to disseminating. Another trend will be real time or machine speed exchange of information that can be evaluated by smarter devices. OpenIOC from Mandiant is one to monitor in this regard; they have technology, methodology and a strong set of customers to enable a sharing network. Their recent corporate combination with FireEye could enable an accelerated sharing of indicators.

- **Cloud Computing and the Internet of Things (IOT):**

Both of these initiatives will have profound effects in both the near and far future and have significant cyber security impact. I have given you a very high level overview below, both areas bear detailed investigation at the technical and strategic level of your organization's future planning.

- **Cloud Computing:** The concept for cloud computing started with timesharing models on ancient mainframes – way back in the 1950s and 1960s. When computing first emerged, the available resources were scarce and very expensive, and making them available to many people on a shared basis was imperative in order to spread the cost over the widest base of users. These systems were local at first, but terminals connected to primitive network circuits could allow access to over a wider area as the technology progressed. As the cost of computing plummeted, organizations added additional machines on an exponential basis, cumulating with the deployment of personal computers to virtually everyone in the organization. Scarcity was replaced with abundance and abundance created a major administrative and maintenance burden along with an increasingly complex portfolio of applications.

- The World Wide Web brought the idea of a shared resource back to the forefront. Google's search engine and Amazon's e-commerce would not have worked without the ability to share large amounts of information across millions of different people and organizations. Another innovation was Software as a Service (SAAS), with Salesforce.com as one of the early innovators. Prior to Salesforce.com, if you wanted to install a Customer Relationship Management System, you had to contract in advance (usually millions of upfront dollars), mobilize the IT team to install and support a major new initiative, and then gradually deploy internal software across your sales and support team. Salesforce.com upended this model, allowing companies to add individual users in their cloud with almost no upfront cost, while allowing growth as demand grew. Operating expense replaced the huge capital expense associated with the enterprise system and payback was accelerated.

Cloud computing is on the cusp of expanding greatly over the coming years and has some profound impacts on computing and security. For organizations, the ability to consume resources based on what is used represents a better model, and in most cases, significantly lower costs. There are definite risks, but I am a strong proponent of cloud computing's security position for the following reasons:

- **Provider expertise:** When you think of cloud providers, you likely think of Microsoft, Amazon, Google, and Rackspace. There are many more and a dizzying array of options: private clouds, hybrid clouds, co-location and Platform as a Service(PAAS) are just a few. In the same way that Walmart's size has given them the edge on retail and logistics system expertise, these providers are building an incredible talent pool of people and capabilities to service their increasingly savvy cloud customers across a wide set of markets. When I compare the security staff of Microsoft Azure with the best teams of people in corporate America, I would likely pick the cloud provider as a long term security partner. The expertise and expense involved with strong cyber defenses can be spread across hundreds or thousands of customers.

- **Newer platform:** One of the biggest security risks we identified in earlier chapters is legacy hardware and software applications that are still being used, despite their age and general lack of security awareness. So far, the cloud providers have resisted, or the market hasn't supported, a wholesale movement of legacy systems to the cloud. Because of the use of newer hardware, current operating systems, and relatively new application software with more security designed in from the start, organizations will get a natural advantage as they move things to the cloud.

- **Increased monitoring:** The cloud is a shared environment and all the vendors are building significant monitoring capabilities that are staffed around the clock. This service comes with even a basic contract for services and enhances the visibility on what is transpiring at any given moment.

- **Increased audit:** Because of the way that cloud providers get paid, they have to be able to track and bill for the use of resources. This collection of information helps to define a very strong audit trail of activity.

- **Financial liability:** The winning cloud providers will be highly capitalized organizations, just like banking leaders today. In the banking sector, JPMorgan Chase can bring economies to bear that a regional bank could only dream of doing. This will also be the case in the cloud and most of the competitors today have very deep pockets in terms of financial assets and insurance. While you don't want to deal with attacks, knowing that there is recourse in the event the cloud provider was breached provides an additional layer of security.

- **Business continuity:** Most major organizations have redundant system plans built into their recovery scenarios. These facilities can be very expensive and difficult to maintain. Cloud providers continue to add extra resources and offer much more seamless recovery options that can cost much less.

The Internet of Things (IOT): The IOT is beginning to emerge as a major growth area for the next 10 years and will become a major pillar in our systems world. The IOT was named in 1999 and is based around uniquely identifiable objects that are connectable to the Internet and other networks that follow. ABI Research has estimated that there will be 30 billion devices connected to the IOT by 2020. There are a host of technologies like RFID (Radio Frequency Identification), NFC (Near Field Communications), and QR (Quick Response codes) that will enable the connection and exchange of data. The newest version of Internet Protocol (IPV6) has been designed to handle trillions of devices with unique identifiers. A car, as a system or collection of objects and subsystems, will have many connection points – the brakes might give off a reading on wear, the engine on operating statistics, the GPS on location statistics and so on. The security implications for this are profound and still under development in many cases.

For passive devices, generating false readings or eliminating communications may be a major problem. On interactive objects, the complexities become much more sinister. In a recent segment of 60 Minutes, former Vice President Dick Cheney was interviewed about the electronic pacemaker that had been keeping him alive prior to a heart transplant. The Vice President outlined the concerns that the Secret Service had turned the Wi-Fi access capability of his pacemaker off, worrying that a hacker could take control of the device remotely, disrupt the his heart activity, and kill him. I'm sure this sounds like a scenario our of a movie, but scenarios like this will be very real in the near future.

Long term predictions – up to 2020: All of the trends for increased attacks could continue to manifest themselves, but my personal opinion is that you will see a decrease in this time frame, especially in the run of the mill, repeatable attacks. I think there will still be very talented hackers that initiate some stunning attacks and critical infrastructure is still greatly at risk, but that industry and government's efforts to work together and share information will start bearing fruit, raising prosecutions and building better defenses.

Here are some long term areas to monitor, continually updating your organization's strategy as they evolve:

- **People:** Great people will be in short supply for the foreseeable future. Despite some great leaps forward in terms of automated defenses, the personnel need will outstrip the available supply. There will be plenty of people that say they are cyber experts, but be careful to validate both character and skills at the hiring point and periodically thereafter. New certificates and online learning will also help to increase the pool of talent. Take good care of your team; in many cases defending the enterprise is a difficult and stressful assignment – well-placed encouragement and recognition for a job well done are in order.

- **Unsupported software:** There are several major software platforms that will be left unsupported by industry, with Microsoft XP and older versions of Java as prime examples. In Microsoft's case, XP has been superseded by several new Windows releases and the company can't justify the effort to keep supporting patches and updates. There might be many reasons why your organization can't move to a better secured platform, but I would warn you that you are raising the risk of an attack by perpetuating old software.

- **Future application software development:** While computer networks are increasingly made up of standardized components (Cisco routers as an example), many organizations will commission unique software applications or continue to develop their own as a means of gaining competitive advantage over their competitors. It is imperative that new applications or upgrades of existing legacy systems incorporate the best security lessons learned. Microsoft has built and deployed the Microsoft Security Development Lifecycle methodology, and there are other very good frameworks for software developers to utilize. ISO (International Standards Organization) 27034 "Information technology – Security techniques – Application security," is designed to be a vendor neutral standard that helps organizations develop and build software that is more secure from the creation – "baking security in" versus "pasting it on top". The ISO standard does not preclude the use of other development lifecycles or methodologies and is being adopted on a worldwide basis.

- **Multi-factor authentication:** You might finally see the end of the username/password combination for credentialing over the next five years, at least for important systems access. The country had a chance to execute a national ID credentialing strategy right after 9/11, but I think it unlikely to happen without a major tragedy at the national level. There are some very good research and development programs and promising technology that will help validate individuals that could go mainstream, especially in the event of a polarizing event. I would love to move to a biometric authentication or some other method that would eliminate managing a trove of strong passwords poorly.

- **Encryption:** Encryption is an important defense element, but has had a history of being difficult to implement and manage. End device encryption of hard drives is the easiest scenario to visualize, with a single, authorized owner providing the decryption key. When you scale this up to thousands or tens of thousands of interactive employees, customers, and web site visitors, the administration and complexity goes up greatly. This is an important area to monitor, particularly in the area of the organization's most important data.

- **Mobile:** Mobile devices will get more secure and uses will fragment into multiple segments ranging from pure consumer to highly secure devices for business and government users. Bring Your Own Device (BYOD) will continue as a trend - the savings and convenience make it too appealing to resist for both individuals and organizations. Tablets will become very intertwined into enterprise systems and care will have to be taken to manage access rights and to avoid storing of critical records locally.

- **Wearable computers:** Google Glass and Samsung SmartWatch are two of the first wearable devices in the marketplace, but I expect you will see a significant increase in the variety and functionality over the next couple of years. I'm personally waiting for the Google Glass functionality integrated into a pair of intelligent contact lenses, but despite some news articles and prototypes, I may have to wait a number of years. Most of the manufacturers will be utilizing existing technology to produce these devices, security should parallel the mobile marketplace and continue to show improvements.

- **Internet of Things (IOT):** Estimates for unique devices connected to networks range from few to many, but all end in billions. There will be many uses that will make economic sense and some breakthrough applications that will change your world. I recently saw a demonstration of some very small devices that could be used to mark and track valuable items – even when stolen, they would periodically report back to a sensor collection device that would pinpoint their location. I used a GPS watch when I trained for the Marine Corps Marathon and the amount of data collected was stunning – but couple that relatively simple device with thousands of sensors and a camera that recognizes important landmarks, air quality, traffic congestion and other elements, and you start to see how the IOT will explode.

- **The disappearing perimeter walls:** Traditional cyber defenses have used a perimeter model, a modern day instantiation of the castle walls. The bad people were kept out through a limited access model and the good allowed to operate freely as a trusted citizen. This metaphor has been eroding quickly and the future trend is for it to diminish even more. You may have islands of security around your critical data, but it's difficult to run a perimeter-based system in today's modern environment.

- **Insurance:** Cyber insurance is evolving rapidly. It is an area where I'm not qualified to compare and contrast the different elements, so I will leave that to another work or update this book with outside insurance expertise at a later date. Suffice to say, your organization should evaluate the tradeoffs of having insurance based on the risk profile you are willing to absorb.

Chapter 10 Key Points Summary:

The future of information technology, cyber threats and cyber defenses are evolving at an incredible pace.

Attacks will continue to mount in sophistication, but the immense amount of work involved in good cyber hygiene will keep the older simpler attack vectors in play, as well. Vigilance is paramount.

Your legacy systems are getting older every year and your information systems environment is getting more complex. New capabilities bolted into a framework of decades old technologies present a challenging problem for security efforts.

Bring Your Own Devices (BYOD) and mobile accesses have emerged and are in great demand as productivity enhancers. Make sure that you are working to prevent the attacks that are enabled by this strategy.

The cloud represents a brand new opportunity (and brings new threats) to upgrade your systems and reduce your overall risk profile.

The Internet of Things (IOT) will provide large amounts of new real time situational awareness monitoring data along with decreasing sensor costs. There will also be new attack vulnerabilities created.

The knowledge base regarding cyber security and threat management is growing rapidly, but unfortunately, it is growing on both the defensive and offensive side of the equation. Your opponents are gearing up quickly to take advantage of any weaknesses.

Your people will continue to be your greatest asset in terms of prevention and response. Hiring, continued vetting, training, and retention are key elements to a security effort.

Monitoring future directions is more than an IT issue – there should be a cross organizational effort to insure that the right blend of new capabilities are incorporated for competitive advantage and efficiency but with the right security questions and risks being assessed.

Chapter 11: Parting Thoughts

*"Life has a way of setting things in order and leaving them be.
Very tidy, is life."* - Jean Anouilh

I hope you have enjoyed the material in this book and found it useful as a tool to improve your understanding and resiliency. I have learned a great deal from the people that I've interviewed and the research I've conducted while creating the material in this book. The desire to minimize cyber threats is a strong drumbeat that is reverberating globally and I think it bodes well for the long term future for the forces of good, or at least, legal.

Here are a few parting personal opinions as you continue your cyber-based adventures:

Common sense counts: Despite all the complexity, many issues and processes come down to someone applying common sense to an approach. There are few issues that can't be simplified enough to allow an adequate decision to be made. Tradeoffs are important to understand.

Discipline: The fight over cyber is a long, sustained effort. There is bound to be fatigue, boredom and periods along the way where your team would rather do anything than look at another set of audit logs or reports. Learning from organizations that have effectively "stood watch" for decades is an important way to avoid some of the risk of "falling asleep at the wheel." It is a hard, but worthwhile, endeavor.

The great is the enemy of the good: I've always wanted perfection, but never obtained it – not even once. I've seen and participated in multi-year programs with ambitious goals – some that worked well and others that were abysmal failures. In most cases, Stephen Covey's admonition to "begin with the end in mind" made the difference between success and failure. Fuzzy objectives failed, where well-articulated and rational targets were achieved. In every success there was a key person making the incremental tradeoffs that move the project toward completion. It is important to get started and to learn on the journey.

Every moment counts: Time passes very quickly and there is no commodity more precious and mercurial. You can buy some with additional people, but only within the limits of your objectives – nine women can't have a baby in one month as outlined by Frederick Brooks in his *Mythical Man-Month* treatise. Have a plan ready to go and practice, practice, practice. When something bad happens, respond like your life depended upon it.

The IT department needs business training: Most of the IT departments I've worked with are hardworking, dedicated people. Studies have shown their need for growth and change are high, but overall social needs are significantly lower than the average employee. It is also the case that many IT groups do not understand the overall mission, structure and tradeoffs being performed in the overall organization. I'd recommend to leadership that they spend time explaining these elements of the organization to insure that the right focus is being applied in the information technology creation and deployment process.

Business people need technical awareness: I am not advocating that everyone in the organization be a coder or take programming classes, but the information highway is so important to every aspect of our organizations, that everyone should have a good understanding of how it works. I've heard many of my colleagues say "just let my kids do it," assuming that if you grew up clicking and texting that you are somehow imparted a vast understanding of the inner workings of technology. This is not the case and organizations should ensure that there is some good overview training in place.

People are critical resources: I've heard a thousand speeches on how important people are to every organization. I've also seen many organizations that don't follow through on the efforts required to get the best out of the people they have, or stop halfway down the organization. I've seen organizations where everyone on the executive team is scheduled down to the last minute, but a walk through the call center or operations center finds many people web surfing or playing solitaire for extended periods. The cyber defense area is mostly a cost to the organization, so efforts should be made to motivate, train, and promote the good people, and weed out the non-performing individuals.

Politics and silos can waste time and money, and subvert overall defenses: I have worked in some very large organizations in my career and seen some tremendous opportunities for teamwork go to waste because of partisan efforts that considered divisional or department benefits over those of the entire organization. In some cases, executive management and the board created this with localized incentives, blithely assuming that nobody would forget the overall objectives. In the cyber defense area, the entire organization is in a common situation, and a united and collaborative front is imperative for preparation and incident response.

Your CSO may be a tremendous cyber asset: If you are a large organization and have a formal physical security program, you may be under-utilizing your Chief Security Officer on the cyber side of the organization. The CSO typically has an extended history of dealing with physical threats of many different natures, minimizing damages, and assessing and responding to incidents. Harnessing this expertise is a vital augmentation to your efforts.

Your castle has 100 windows: Charles Jennings and Lori Fena published a book well ahead of its time called *The Hundredth Window*. It dealt with the early issues of computer security and privacy. The key premise holds true today – if you have 100 windows and 99 of them are locked, you are 100% vulnerable through the open window, not 99% secure.

The U.S. government is not agile: Despite the efforts of many dedicated civil servants, military officers and political appointees, the U.S. government is mostly hopeless when it comes to a rapid coordinated response to a large problem. It may be a function of our political system and all the safeguards that the founders built into the Constitution, but my personal opinion is that size kills agility and responsiveness in the best of large organizations, and government has none of the profit urgency that refocuses corporations when they lose their way. Short of a terrible event, I don't see a lot of agility and inspired capabilities emerging.

Kudos and raves: The following organizations have proven to me to be very good in the missions that they support or the products/services they provide:

- **NACD (National Association of Corporate Directors):** The NACD, headquartered in Washington D.C. is an excellent organization with a wide range of services aimed at the board of directors' increasingly complex role. The website is www.nacdonline.org and they have a wide range of services, seminars, and training that can help directors improve their capabilities, share information, and meet their peers. They have a national meeting annually and individual chapters across the country also host a wide range of local events. Highly recommended if you are a director or want to be one in the future.

- **OASIS (Organization for the Advancement of Structured Information Standards):** I have been a member of OASIS for years and been thoroughly impressed with their accomplishments, structure, and people. The organization works on a wide array of standards. These standards, as outlined in one of the previous chapters, can revolutionize the way information is created and disseminated. Common Alerting Protocol (CAP) has been the main standard I've been involved with, and it's gone from obscurity to worldwide use in 10 years. Their website is www.oasis-open.org. They are worth an evaluation by your organization. Another key differentiator is that OASIS standards are free to access and use once created, unlike ISO standards that are looking for money each time the documents are sold.

- **SANS Institute:** The SANS Institute (www.sans.org) was established in 1989 as a cooperative research and education organization. Its programs now reach more than 165,000 security professionals around the world. I listed their top 20 cyber security controls in a previous chapter, but those excellent guidelines are only the tip of the iceberg of what SANS can provide your organization.

- **Global Risk Network (GRN):** The Global Risk Network is part of New York University (NYU). Their website is http://www.nyu.edu/intercep/grn/. Members of the GRN collaborate on major risk topics faced by large, global organizations. Example organizations are Barclays, Deutsche Bank, GardaWorld, Goldman Sachs, Guardian Life Insurance Co., Indy Racing League, JetBlue Airways, Lancers Network Limited, Microsoft, Novartis Institutes for BioMedical Research, Inc., Palantir Technologies, Pfizer, Pinkerton / Securitas, Prudential, RBS Group, Royal Bank of Scotland, Simudyne, Thomson Reuters, and Vodafone. They do face-to-face meetings and communicate a wide variety of information on an ongoing basis. If your organization is multi-national in nature, I have found them very useful.

- **Microsoft:** I'm a big Microsoft fan, especially now that they are getting a new CEO. In my lifetime, I've seen this company change the computing game on a global basis. When I compare my two pound laptop with 100GB of storage to my first IBM PC with two floppy disk drives, the acceleration of technology really hits home. My prediction is that Microsoft will continue to dominate the back office part of computing, making the infrastructure a more secure and scalable environment. Their Azure cloud has tremendous promise for enhancing security. I hope this confidence is supported – we will all benefit if the company performs.

- **Cisco:** Cisco is one of the pillars of the networked world. They are an innovative company with a fantastic reputation for deep thinking and integration into today's world of technology. They've had a few fits and starts with trying to be a consumer company, but their big system expertise and product set is one that I've counted on for many years. I expect they will continue to improve into the future and be one of your key vendors.

- **Intel:** Intel used to be on the front page of every PC and IT magazine all the time – of course, this was back when front pages were made of paper! Their processors powered the PC and Internet generation, increasing price/performance at a stunning rate defined by Moore's law over a period that defies imagination. Recently, they have been instrumental in a chip called the TPM (Trusted Platform Module), which when fully incorporated into future systems architecture, will help security activities greatly.

- **The Giving Pledge:** Little to do with cybersecurity, but worthy of recognition is the vast amount of wealth that affluent individuals worldwide are dedicating to humanity rather than their heirs. Started by the Bill and Melinda Gates Foundation and supported by Warren Buffet, this effort has generated worldwide attention and set the stage for many good things happening now and in the future.

Frustration points: There are many areas where progress around cyber is being stymied, sabotaged, or blocked. Some of these efforts are calculated, some are sheer incompetence, and others are political. While it might feel good to rant, it will not help the situation, so I would encourage you to make as many constructive efforts as possible, and work toward better cyber defenses with everyone who is working toward the same objectives.

Chapter 11 Key Points Summary:

The world will get beyond the current state of cyber threats and cyber will become a more manageable risk for organizations. This may take a long time.

There will always need to be a vigilant approach to security, both physical and in the cyber arena.

Information sharing will continue to evolve and hit the mainstream in the next few years. It will likely be driven by the private sector versus government.

There will be winners and losers worldwide in the race to provide good solutions - keep validating that your defenses are from the leaders.

Despite all the technology changes, the basic nature of human beings is not going to change, so all defenses and security must take this into account. Passive cyber security, like the progression from lap belts to shoulder harnesses to front airbags to multiple airbags in vehicles will help, but deliberate attacks and accidents will happen. Be prepared.

Appendix A: Simple Cyber Hygiene Items

There are many different defenses and actions your organization can take to make itself more prepared and ready for an attack – some very complicated and too time consuming to implement. There are also some very simple steps you can monitor to ensure that you are doing the basics to protect your organization. Some of these will sound incredibly simplistic and you'll have a hard time understanding how they wouldn't be second nature, but many intrusions are accomplished through simple methods that could have easily been remedied in advance.

Strong passwords: There was recent breach where a large website's user data was stolen and significant amounts of it posted on the web. Through some innovative work, some individuals were able to decrypt the passwords utilized and the results were stunning – "password" and "12345" were still highly prevalent, even after all the years of cyber awareness. Make sure your organization is enforcing a decent password length.

Enforced password changes: I'd recommend for at least your critical applications that you enforce a regular change cycle in strong passwords. It is painful for everyone involved, and there is a corresponding support burden that goes with this activity, but it could cut off an attacker prematurely from compromising your systems.

Eliminating departed employees/contractors/suppliers: No matter how friendly a termination, people's login credentials leaving the organization must be deleted/eliminated from the overall security system. This is usually a straightforward personnel issue, but gets cloudy with contractors and suppliers that may be given credentials outside the employee system.

Generic accounts: Some organizations set up system accounts that are used by many different people for access. This type of credential can open a window to an intruder, especially if the password is not changed frequently. That particular account might not give any special access, but it could be connected to other vital systems, or give an intruder insight into a password that is used for many different accounts inside the organization.

Patching known vulnerabilities/updating malware signatures: The major providers issue regular security patches that will hinder attacks from known vulnerabilities that have been discovered, analysed and fixed. You should ensure your organization is applying these updates on a disciplined basis. There may be risk trade-offs involved, depending on your stable of legacy systems, but this is an important activity.

Downloading massive customer files to traveling mobile devices: There are many processes that depend on individuals using Excel or another application to analyse customer data. When these processes migrate outside the building, the risk of an advertent data breach goes up greatly – do a search on lost equipment if you need to confirm. Attachments to email can be another devastating way of pushing important information into unprotected access areas.

Changing default device passwords: New devices like network switches and routers typically come with a default password so that they can be accessed immediately by systems personnel doing the installation. It is critical to have a process to insure that the default password is changed and not replaced with another organization wide default password.

Checking logs: You likely have defensive systems in place that are continually monitoring your network and other activities. It is critical to have a process to audit and correct issues identified in these logs. Some can be incredibly dense and it is easy to ignore with the many other things a security or network analyst has to do.

Data destruction on obsolete equipment: When you take a laptop or a system drive or a network drive or any other device out of service, your organization needs to ensure that the equipment has been scrubbed of any useful information. This certainly includes organizational data, but also password files, configuration files and many other pieces of data that, in the wrong hands, could open a window and allow a breach.

Limit physical access: An organization can be affected in a lot of ways, but one of the easiest is through a physical USB device containing malware being plugged into one of your computers. This is difficult to police completely, but keeping access to a minimum and following basic precautions (locked doors, access logs, etc.) can go a long way toward preventing unauthorized intrusions.

Limit and/or segregate network access: Many organizations have visitors who need access to the internet and their systems while inside your organization's facilities. Establishing a completely separate Internet access point that is not connected in any way to your network is a far safer method than trying to carve out a secured portion of your network for visitors.

Require background checks and insurance from your vendors: You may have significant threats working in your facility through an outsourced janitorial, maintenance, or construction vendor. Make sure you are contractually covered for these potential vulnerabilities.

Know where your information is: You may be taking a very proactive approach toward protecting your organization's data and preparing a response to all anticipated attacks on your network or enterprise systems, but your responsibility may not end at the organization's physical limits. Be sure to identify all the places where sensitive information might be stored; in today's digital environment you may have copies of information at your attorney's office, outside vendors, processing partners or many other potential locations. Insure that they are all being identified and protected adequately.

Appendix B: Sample Incident Response Checklist

Department of Justice: DOJ issued an excellent, comprehensive document on August 6, 2013 that is available in its entirety on the web at http://www.justice.gov/opcl/breach-procedures.pdf   I've included the table of contents for you to look at the extent of the thinking required for a federal agency to respond to a data breach:

SOURCE: DOJ Breach Procedure

Appendix C: Executive Order on Cyber and NIST Framework

This appendix provides some reference information that is important to have a general knowledge about and to follow the evolving efforts of the U.S. federal government.

The White House

Office of the Press Secretary

For Immediate Release
February 12, 2013

EXECUTIVE ORDER

- - - - - - -

IMPROVING CRITICAL INFRASTRUCTURE CYBERSECURITY

By the authority vested in me as President by the Constitution and the laws of the United States of America, it is hereby ordered as follows:

Section 1. Policy. Repeated cyber intrusions into critical infrastructure demonstrate the need for improved cybersecurity. The cyber threat to critical infrastructure continues to grow and represents one of the most serious national security challenges we must confront. The national and economic security of the United States depends on the reliable functioning of the Nation's critical infrastructure in the face of such threats. It is the policy of the United States to enhance the security and resilience of the Nation's critical infrastructure and to maintain a cyber environment that encourages efficiency, innovation, and economic prosperity while promoting safety, security, business confidentiality, privacy, and civil liberties. We can achieve these goals through a partnership with the owners and operators of critical infrastructure to improve cybersecurity information sharing and collaboratively develop and implement risk-based standards.

Sec. 2. Critical Infrastructure. As used in this order, the term critical infrastructure means systems and assets, whether physical or virtual, so vital to the United States that the incapacity or destruction of such systems and assets would have a debilitating impact on security, national economic security, national public health or safety, or any combination of those matters.

Sec. 3. Policy Coordination. Policy coordination, guidance, dispute resolution, and periodic in-progress reviews for the functions and programs described and assigned herein shall be provided through the interagency process established in Presidential Policy Directive-1 of February 13, 2009 (Organization of the National Security Council System), or any successor.

Sec. 4. Cybersecurity Information Sharing. (a) It is the policy of the United States Government to increase the volume, timeliness, and quality of cyber threat information shared with U.S. private sector entities so that these entities may better protect and defend themselves against cyber threats. Within 120 days of the date of this order, the Attorney General, the Secretary of Homeland Security (the "Secretary"), and the Director of National Intelligence shall each issue instructions consistent with their authorities and with the requirements of section 12(c) of this order to ensure the timely production of unclassified reports of cyber threats to the U.S. homeland that identify a specific targeted entity. The instructions shall address the need to protect intelligence and law enforcement sources, methods, operations, and investigations.

(b) The Secretary and the Attorney General, in coordination with the Director of National Intelligence, shall establish a process that rapidly disseminates the reports produced pursuant to section 4(a) of this order to the targeted entity. Such process shall also, consistent with the need to protect national security information, include the dissemination of classified reports to critical infrastructure entities authorized to receive them. The Secretary and the Attorney General, in coordination with the Director of National Intelligence, shall establish a system for tracking the production, dissemination, and disposition of these reports.

(c) To assist the owners and operators of critical infrastructure in protecting their systems from unauthorized access, exploitation, or harm, the Secretary, consistent with 6 U.S.C. 143 and in collaboration with the Secretary of Defense, shall, within 120 days of the date of this order, establish procedures to expand the Enhanced Cybersecurity Services program to all critical infrastructure sectors. This voluntary information sharing program will provide classified cyber threat and technical information from the Government to eligible critical infrastructure companies or commercial service providers that offer security services to critical infrastructure.

(d) The Secretary, as the Executive Agent for the Classified National Security Information Program created under Executive Order 13549 of August 18, 2010 (Classified National Security Information Program for State, Local, Tribal, and Private Sector Entities), shall expedite the processing of security clearances to appropriate personnel employed by critical infrastructure owners and operators, prioritizing the critical infrastructure identified in section 9 of this order.

(e) In order to maximize the utility of cyber threat information sharing with the private sector, the Secretary shall expand the use of programs that bring private sector subject-matter experts into Federal service on a temporary basis. These subject matter experts should provide advice regarding the content, structure, and types of information most useful to critical infrastructure owners and operators in reducing and mitigating cyber risks.

Sec. 5. Privacy and Civil Liberties Protections. (a) Agencies shall coordinate their activities under this order with their senior agency officials for privacy and civil liberties and ensure that privacy and civil liberties protections are incorporated into such activities. Such protections shall be based upon the Fair Information Practice Principles and other privacy and civil liberties policies, principles, and frameworks as they apply to each agency's activities.

(b) The Chief Privacy Officer and the Officer for Civil Rights and Civil Liberties of the Department of Homeland Security (DHS) shall assess the privacy and civil liberties risks of the functions and programs undertaken by DHS as called for in this order and shall recommend to the Secretary ways to minimize or mitigate such risks, in a publicly available report, to be released within 1 year of the date of this order. Senior agency privacy and civil liberties officials for other agencies engaged in activities under this order shall conduct assessments of their agency activities and provide those assessments to DHS for consideration and inclusion in the report. The report shall be reviewed on an annual basis and revised as necessary. The report may contain a classified annex if necessary. Assessments shall include evaluation of activities against the Fair Information Practice Principles and other applicable privacy and civil liberties policies, principles, and frameworks. Agencies shall consider the assessments and

197

recommendations of the report in implementing privacy and civil liberties protections for agency activities.

(c) In producing the report required under subsection (b) of this section, the Chief Privacy Officer and the Officer for Civil Rights and Civil Liberties of DHS shall consult with the Privacy and Civil Liberties Oversight Board and coordinate with the Office of Management and Budget (OMB).

(d) Information submitted voluntarily in accordance with 6 U.S.C. 133 by private entities under this order shall be protected from disclosure to the fullest extent permitted by law.

Sec. 6. Consultative Process. The Secretary shall establish a consultative process to coordinate improvements to the cybersecurity of critical infrastructure. As part of the consultative process, the Secretary shall engage and consider the advice, on matters set forth in this order, of the Critical Infrastructure Partnership Advisory Council; Sector Coordinating Councils; critical infrastructure owners and operators; Sector-Specific Agencies; other relevant agencies; independent regulatory agencies; State, local, territorial, and tribal governments; universities; and outside experts.

Sec. 7. Baseline Framework to Reduce Cyber Risk to Critical Infrastructure. (a) The Secretary of Commerce shall direct the Director of the National Institute of Standards and Technology (the "Director") to lead the development of a framework to reduce cyber risks to critical infrastructure (the "Cybersecurity Framework"). The Cybersecurity Framework shall include a set of standards, methodologies, procedures, and processes that align policy, business, and technological approaches to address cyber risks. The Cybersecurity Framework shall incorporate voluntary consensus standards and industry best practices to the fullest extent possible. The Cybersecurity Framework shall be consistent with voluntary international standards when such international standards will advance the objectives of this order, and shall meet the requirements of the National Institute of Standards and Technology Act, as amended (15 U.S.C. 271 et seq.), the National Technology Transfer and Advancement Act of 1995 (Public Law 104-113), and OMB Circular A-119, as revised.

(b) The Cybersecurity Framework shall provide a prioritized, flexible, repeatable, performance-based, and cost-effective approach, including information security measures and controls, to help owners and operators of critical infrastructure identify, assess, and manage cyber risk. The Cybersecurity Framework shall focus on identifying cross-sector security standards and guidelines applicable to critical infrastructure. The Cybersecurity Framework will also identify areas for improvement that should be addressed through future collaboration with particular sectors and standards-developing organizations. To enable technical innovation and account for organizational differences, the Cybersecurity Framework will provide guidance that is technology neutral and that enables critical infrastructure sectors to benefit from a competitive market for products and services that meet the standards, methodologies, procedures, and processes developed to address cyber risks. The Cybersecurity Framework shall include guidance for measuring the performance of an entity in implementing the Cybersecurity Framework.

(c) The Cybersecurity Framework shall include methodologies to identify and mitigate impacts of the Cybersecurity Framework and associated information security measures or controls on business confidentiality, and to protect individual privacy and civil liberties.

(d) In developing the Cybersecurity Framework, the Director shall engage in an open public review and comment process. The Director shall also consult with the Secretary, the National Security Agency, Sector-Specific Agencies and other interested agencies including OMB, owners and operators of critical infrastructure, and other stakeholders through the consultative process established in section 6 of this order. The Secretary, the Director of National Intelligence, and the heads of other relevant agencies shall provide threat and vulnerability information and technical expertise to inform the development of the Cybersecurity Framework. The Secretary shall provide performance goals for the Cybersecurity Framework informed by work under section 9 of this order.

(e) Within 240 days of the date of this order, the Director shall publish a preliminary version of the Cybersecurity Framework (the "preliminary Framework"). Within 1 year of the date of this order, and after coordination with the Secretary to ensure suitability under section 8 of this order, the Director shall publish a final version of the Cybersecurity Framework (the "final Framework").

(f) Consistent with statutory responsibilities, the Director will ensure the Cybersecurity Framework and related guidance is reviewed and updated as necessary, taking into consideration technological changes, changes in cyber risks, operational feedback from owners and operators of critical infrastructure, experience from the implementation of section 8 of this order, and any other relevant factors.

Sec. 8. Voluntary Critical Infrastructure Cybersecurity Program. (a) The Secretary, in coordination with Sector-Specific Agencies, shall establish a voluntary program to support the adoption of the Cybersecurity Framework by owners and operators of critical infrastructure and any other interested entities (the "Program").

(b) Sector-Specific Agencies, in consultation with the Secretary and other interested agencies, shall coordinate with the Sector Coordinating Councils to review the Cybersecurity Framework and, if necessary, develop implementation guidance or supplemental materials to address sector-specific risks and operating environments.

(c) Sector-Specific Agencies shall report annually to the President, through the Secretary, on the extent to which owners and operators notified under section 9 of this order are participating in the Program.

(d) The Secretary shall coordinate establishment of a set of incentives designed to promote participation in the Program. Within 120 days of the date of this order, the Secretary and the Secretaries of the Treasury and Commerce each shall make recommendations separately to the President, through the Assistant to the President for Homeland Security and Counterterrorism and the Assistant to the President for Economic Affairs, that shall include analysis of the benefits and relative effectiveness of such incentives, and whether the incentives would require legislation or can be provided under existing law and authorities to participants in the Program.

(e) Within 120 days of the date of this order, the Secretary of Defense and the Administrator of General Services, in consultation with the Secretary and the Federal Acquisition Regulatory Council, shall make recommendations to the President, through the Assistant to the President for Homeland Security and Counterterrorism and the Assistant to the President for Economic Affairs, on the feasibility, security benefits, and relative merits of incorporating security standards into acquisition planning and contract administration. The report shall address what steps can be taken to harmonize and make consistent existing procurement requirements related to cybersecurity.

Sec. 9. Identification of Critical Infrastructure at Greatest Risk. (a) Within 150 days of the date of this order, the Secretary shall use a risk-based approach to identify critical infrastructure where a cybersecurity incident could reasonably result in catastrophic regional or national effects on public health or safety, economic security, or national security. In identifying critical infrastructure for this purpose, the Secretary shall use the consultative process established in section 6 of this order and draw upon the expertise of Sector-Specific Agencies. The Secretary shall apply consistent, objective criteria in identifying such critical infrastructure. The Secretary shall not identify any commercial information technology products or consumer information technology services under this section. The Secretary shall review and update the list of identified critical infrastructure under this section on an annual basis, and provide such list to the President, through the Assistant to the President for Homeland Security and Counterterrorism and the Assistant to the President for Economic Affairs.

(b) Heads of Sector-Specific Agencies and other relevant agencies shall provide the Secretary with information necessary to carry out the responsibilities under this section. The Secretary shall develop a process for other relevant stakeholders to submit information to assist in making the identifications required in subsection (a) of this section.

(c) The Secretary, in coordination with Sector-Specific Agencies, shall confidentially notify owners and operators of critical infrastructure identified under subsection (a) of this section that they have been so identified, and ensure identified owners and operators are provided the basis for the determination. The Secretary shall establish a process through which owners and operators of critical infrastructure may submit relevant information and request reconsideration of identifications under subsection (a) of this section.

Sec. 10. Adoption of Framework. (a) Agencies with responsibility for regulating the security of critical infrastructure shall engage in a consultative process with DHS, OMB, and the National Security Staff to review the preliminary Cybersecurity Framework and determine if current cybersecurity regulatory requirements are sufficient given current and projected risks. In making such determination, these agencies shall consider the identification of critical infrastructure required under section 9 of this order. Within 90 days of the publication of the preliminary Framework, these agencies shall submit a report to the President, through the Assistant to the President for Homeland Security and Counterterrorism, the Director of OMB, and the Assistant to the President for Economic Affairs, that states whether or not the agency has clear authority to establish requirements based upon the Cybersecurity Framework to sufficiently address current and projected cyber risks to critical infrastructure, the existing authorities identified, and any additional authority required.

(b) If current regulatory requirements are deemed to be insufficient, within 90 days of publication of the final Framework, agencies identified in subsection (a) of this section shall propose prioritized, risk-based, efficient, and coordinated actions, consistent with Executive Order 12866 of September 30, 1993 (Regulatory Planning and Review), Executive Order 13563 of January 18, 2011 (Improving Regulation and Regulatory Review), and Executive Order 13609 of May 1, 2012 (Promoting International Regulatory Cooperation), to mitigate cyber risk.

(c) Within 2 years after publication of the final Framework, consistent with Executive Order 13563 and Executive Order 13610 of May 10, 2012 (Identifying and Reducing Regulatory Burdens), agencies identified in subsection (a) of this section shall, in consultation with owners and operators of critical infrastructure, report to OMB on any critical infrastructure subject to ineffective, conflicting, or excessively burdensome cybersecurity requirements. This report shall describe efforts made by agencies, and make recommendations for further actions, to minimize or eliminate such requirements.

(d) The Secretary shall coordinate the provision of technical assistance to agencies identified in subsection (a) of this section on the development of their cybersecurity workforce and programs.

(e) Independent regulatory agencies with responsibility for regulating the security of critical infrastructure are encouraged to engage in a consultative process with the Secretary, relevant Sector-Specific Agencies, and other affected parties to consider prioritized actions to mitigate cyber risks for critical infrastructure consistent with their authorities.

Sec. 11. Definitions. (a) "Agency" means any authority of the United States that is an "agency" under 44 U.S.C. 3502(1), other than those considered to be independent regulatory agencies, as defined in 44 U.S.C. 3502(5).

(b) "Critical Infrastructure Partnership Advisory Council" means the council established by DHS under 6 U.S.C. 451 to facilitate effective interaction and coordination of critical infrastructure protection activities among the Federal Government; the private sector; and State, local, territorial, and tribal governments.

(c) "Fair Information Practice Principles" means the eight principles set forth in Appendix A of the National Strategy for Trusted Identities in Cyberspace.

(d) "Independent regulatory agency" has the meaning given the term in 44 U.S.C. 3502(5).

(e) "Sector Coordinating Council" means a private sector coordinating council composed of representatives of owners and operators within a particular sector of critical infrastructure established by the National Infrastructure Protection Plan or any successor.

(f) "Sector-Specific Agency" has the meaning given the term in Presidential Policy Directive-21 of February 12, 2013 (Critical Infrastructure Security and Resilience), or any successor.

Sec. 12. General Provisions. (a) This order shall be implemented consistent with applicable law and subject to the availability of appropriations. Nothing in this order shall be construed to provide an agency with authority for regulating the security of critical infrastructure in addition to or to a greater extent than the authority the agency has under existing law. Nothing in this order shall be construed to alter or limit any authority or responsibility of an agency under existing law.

(b) Nothing in this order shall be construed to impair or otherwise affect the functions of the Director of OMB relating to budgetary, administrative, or legislative proposals.

(c) All actions taken pursuant to this order shall be consistent with requirements and authorities to protect intelligence and law enforcement sources and methods. Nothing in this order shall be interpreted to supersede measures established under authority of law to protect the security and integrity of specific activities and associations that are in direct support of intelligence and law enforcement operations.

(d) This order shall be implemented consistent with U.S. international obligations.

(e) This order is not intended to, and does not, create any right or benefit, substantive or procedural, enforceable at law or in equity by any party against the United States, its departments, agencies, or entities, its officers, employees, or agents, or any other person.

BARACK OBAMA

NIST Preliminary Framework:

NIST has issues a preliminary cybersecurity framework - http://www.nist.gov/itl/upload/preliminary-cybersecurity-framework.pdf

NIST has released its final cybersecurity framework for critical infrastructure as of mid-February 2014. I've read it end to end, and for most readers of this book, I doubt it will add to your understanding of the problem unless you are a very detailed IT executive or network manager. There are some very detailed cross references to standards and documents, but practical advice seems limited to me. You can look at www.NIST.gov, or do a simple search on "NIST Cybersecurity Framework." Keep in mind that the framework is based on voluntary cooperation across the public and private sectors; no federal legislation has been passed by the Congress since 2002, despite numerous proposals. Some of the agencies have issued regulations concerning cyber security, but there is much work remaining to have a somewhat cohesive way forward.

Dedication and Acknowledgements

This book is dedicated to Pamela Angelus - thank you for your loving support and encouragement during this effort and always!

In memory of David O'Dell, Barbara O'Dell and Jim James, brother, sister, and great friend, all recently departed and greatly missed.

Christine Scott did a fantastic job editing my final text – and in the most positive way possible.

I've met with a large number of people in the research and creation of this book – cyber security is a topic on many people's mind. I've gotten great feedback and insights on the problems of today and the direction for tomorrow. I hope that I have recognized everyone in this list!

A warm "Thank You" goes out to:
Eric Angelus, Neil Evans, Richard Cauchon, Sherry Lamoreaux, Scott Johnson, Robert Dodge, Charles Jennings, Andy Shapiro, Reed Stager, Annie Searle, Fred Pursell, Andy Padawer, Dan Downing, John Mohr, Elysa Jones, Doug Wilson, Jen Weedon, Kathleen Moriarty, Mark Davidson, Sean Barnum, David Stephenson, Andy Padawer, Eric Kutner, Christopher Karsberg, Graham Plaster, Glenn Kirbo, Lynwood Bishop, David Bray, John Ballantine, Steven Kalan, Jim Traweek, Robert Quinn, Jeff Frazier, Chuck Gottschalk, Liane Pelletier, Johan Wikman, William Schroeder, Anne Castleton, Paul Ketrick, Peter Higgins, Ken Spedden, Hyuk Byun, Bernie Wedge, Joseph Nocera, Gerry Czarnecki, Carolyn Chin, Marcus Sachs, Dean DeBiase, the entire staff of the National Association of Corporate Directors Annual Meeting.

One Last Thing...

If you like this book, please review it and recommend it.

If I missed any great resources that should be known, send them to me and I'll update the electronic version frequently.

If you find errors, omissions, strong points of agreement or disagreement, please let me know. Your opinion matters greatly to me.

If I can help your organization to strategize, prepare, respond or recover; give me a call or send an email. My response time is good in most cases and I handle ambiguity well.

All the best,

Pete ODell
Peterlodell@gmail.com
202 460 9207

INDEX

Made in the USA
Middletown, DE
15 March 2015